The Philosophy of Customary Law

The Philosophy of Customary Law

JAMES BERNARD MURPHY

OXFORD
UNIVERSITY PRESS

OXFORD
UNIVERSITY PRESS

Oxford University Press is a department of the University of Oxford. It furthers the University's objective of excellence in research, scholarship, and education by publishing worldwide.

Oxford New York
Auckland Cape Town Dar es Salaam Hong Kong Karachi Kuala Lumpur Madrid Melbourne Mexico City Nairobi New Delhi Shanghai Taipei Toronto

With offices in
Argentina Austria Brazil Chile Czech Republic France Greece Guatemala Hungary Italy Japan Poland Portugal Singapore South Korea Switzerland Thailand Turkey Ukraine Vietnam

Published in the United States of America by
Oxford University Press
198 Madison Avenue, New York, NY 10016

Library of Congress Cataloging-in-Publication Data

Murphy, James Bernard, 1958-
The philosophy of customary law / James Bernard Murphy.
pages cm
Includes bibliographical references and index.
ISBN 978-0-19-937062-7 ((hardback)
1. Customary law. 2. Customary law—Philosophy. I. Title.
K282.M87 2014
340.501—dc23
2013036301

Note to Readers

This publication is designed to provide accurate and authoritative information in regard to the subject matter covered. It is based upon sources believed to be accurate and reliable and is intended to be current as of the time it was written. It is sold with the understanding that the publisher is not engaged in rendering legal, accounting, or other professional services. If legal advice or other expert assistance is required, the services of a competent professional person should be sought. Also, to confirm that the information has not been affected or changed by recent developments, traditional legal research techniques should be used, including checking primary sources where appropriate.

(Based on the Declaration of Principles jointly adopted by a Committee of the American Bar Association and a Committee of Publishers and Associations.)

In Memoriam
Amanda Perreau-Saussine de Ezcurra

TABLE OF CONTENTS

PREFACE

Although we live in a sea of customs, like the fish, we are not aware of the sea around us. That is why we depend upon foreigners to describe our customs to us, as Tocqueville so memorably did for us Americans in the 1830s. As a French aristocrat, he could see the democratic customs that were invisible to us. Tragically, we often become aware of the power and importance of custom only when custom frustrates our projects for social transformation, whether in Iraq or at home. Customs are the by-product of individual actions but not the project of individual design. Like life itself, customs are what happen when we were making other plans.

Despite their obvious importance to social and political life, custom and customary law have largely escaped philosophical scrutiny. There are important recent book-length philosophical analyses of habit and of convention, but none of custom. The reason, I think, is clear: custom cannot be understood until it is analyzed into the more basic concepts of habit and convention. So a sound theory of custom will have to build upon philosophical accounts of habit and convention. Theorists of social order have also neglected custom, which defies the usual dichotomy of natural order or deliberately stipulated order. Social practices, for example, are usually said to be by nature or by convention. Thus, custom is usually shoehorned into that dichotomy as "second nature" or as "unwritten law." We shall subject these analogies to critical scrutiny. Custom arises neither wholly by nature nor wholly by convention. But perhaps the most fundamental reason for the neglect of custom among philosophers is the sense that custom is, fundamentally, congealed irrationality. But, as Gadamer argued against Habermas, these philosophers ignore the ways in which reason itself rests upon customs of rational inquiry. Reason has a history;

reason is a tradition. This does not imply that reason is only a tradition. Moreover, the kinds of public deliberation that many philosophers associate with democratic politics clearly rest upon many touchstones of customary belief in any particular society. Productive disagreement always rests upon deep grounds of agreement, and those grounds of agreement are the product of custom. Opposing reason to custom is as misleading as opposing reason to emotion: customs, like emotions, are usually congealed reasons. Customs without reason are blind, but reason uncongealed in emotion and custom is impotent.

Many jurists and legal philosophers have their own reasons for neglecting custom and customary law. Ever since Roman lawyers relegated custom to the status of a minor "source" of law, many jurists have focused only on those marginal departments of municipal law (mainly aspects of the mercantile law) in which informal custom is routinely enforced by courts of law. Moreover, the whole notion that custom serves only as a "source" of legal norms is deeply misleading. Are we to suppose that once custom provides the raw material for a legal norm, its job is done? But this relegation of custom to a particular and minor source of municipal law ignores the ways in which custom shapes the interpretation of law. Logically, there cannot be explicit rules for the interpretation and application of rules—without generating a regress. So the interpretation and application of legal rules draws mainly on the customs of the court. This is especially clear in the interpretation of legal standards such as "reasonable man" or "best practice." As the jurists of the historical school argue, if legal rules and principles are not taken up into customary practices, they are likely to lose their effectiveness and, as we shall see, their validity. For many jurists, the doctrine of desuetude marks this essential distinction between legal rules and moral rules: a moral rule remains valid even if ignored by everyone; but a legal rule ignored by everyone falls into desuetude and loses its validity. So legal rules, unlike moral rules, are held hostage to customary usage. However, Hans Kelsen rejects this traditional view: he argues that moral norms can fall into desuetude just as do legal norms. For Kelsen, custom truly is sovereign over both morality and law.[1]

As we shall see, Thomas Aquinas argues that custom interprets and abolishes law, as well as being a source of law. Criminal law is often said to be the least reliant on custom: it is a basic requirement of justice that

---

1. Kelsen says that the moral norm "love your enemies" would remain valid even if most people did not observe it, so long as people generally disapprove of those who hate their enemies. See *Allgemeine Theorie der Normen* ed. Kurt Ringhofer and Robert Walter (Wein: Manzsche, 1979), 139 and 180. Here Kelsen emphasizes customary convictions rather than mere customary usage.

criminal penalties be officially promulgated.[2] Yet, Lynn Mather persuasively shows that basic distinctions between misdemeanors and felonies are routinely made on the basis of the customs of the court, with no basis in statutes.[3] Custom even interprets criminal law. H.L.A. Hart famously argued that custom consists wholly of primary rules, with no secondary rules to govern the creation, modification, and revocation of those primary rules. By contrast, law, says Hart, is a union of primary rules of conduct and secondary rules. But rather than seeing law and custom as alternative and mutually exclusive modes of social regulation, I think it more illuminating to see law as a set of secondary rules governing custom. Law is how custom regulates its own evolution. The Roman jurists used to say that we turn to custom only "cum deficit lex," that is, to make up for the deficiencies of law. But in a wider sense, the rule of law is necessary only "cum deficit consuetudo," to make up for the deficiencies of custom. Where customs clash, evolve too slowly, are vague, or fall short of our ideals, we need law.

By contrast to municipal law, custom is universally treated as a major source of international law; yet, the grounds for the legal force of customary international law are hotly contested. Traditionally, international lawyers have contrasted mere customary usage with a subjective endorsement of that usage as legally binding. In this view, custom has both an objective dimension, namely, sheer usage, and a subjective dimension reflected in the consent or endorsement of the custom by an agent. Sometimes customary practice and state endorsement diverge: for example, many states practice torture yet virtually all states are parties to conventions condemning torture. So is the ban on torture part of customary international law? Are customary international norms binding from mere usage or from the endorsement of states? Or are they binding from a combination of usage and endorsement? Does it even make sense to contrast mere usage with explicit endorsement? Is there such a thing as mere usage?[4] In what sense can agents, whether persons or states, be said to consent to or endorse their own customs? Do we have reasons to conform to custom quite apart from consent? These are issues we shall explore.

---

2. In his recent jurisprudence of customary law, Bederman says, "no one seriously advocates that unofficial and unenacted norms should be the basis of substantive criminal liability in any society." *Custom as a Source of Law* (Cambridge: Cambridge University Press, 2010) 174.

3. Mather, *Plea Bargaining or Trial?: The Process of Criminal-Case Disposition* (Lexington, MA: D. C. Heath, 1979).

4. For an effective critique of the view that customs are the sum of objective usage and subjective endorsement, see Gerald J. Postema "Custom, Normative Practice, and the Law," in *Duke Law Journal* 62: 707–738 (2012).

Perhaps no issue is more fundamental and more contentious than the question of the relation of custom to liberty. Ever since Aristotle, some philosophers and jurists have argued that custom is the mode of regulation of social life most compatible with human freedom. Aristotle says that while laws depend upon force, customs rule invisibly by becoming a second nature. The ancient poet Pindar says that "custom is king"—to which Chrysostom adds "and law is a tyrant."[5] For many theorists, custom is a gentle and easy yoke compared to the frightening coercive apparatus of law. Ancient Roman jurists and traditional common lawyers took custom to be a bulwark of liberty precisely because it was resistant to deliberate political manipulation. The Roman jurists argued that our customs reflect our free consent just as much as do our votes. But other philosophers and jurists, especially Bentham and Mill, have insisted, quite to the contrary, that custom is a tyrant. The fact that we often do not even notice, let alone reject, our customs makes this form of tyranny all the more insidious.

Similarly, many theorists, beginning with the Roman jurists, argue that custom reflects democratic sovereignty because, unlike laws imposed from above, customs arise from below. These philosophers and jurists argue that practice is the best evidence of consent. Hobbes said that a sovereign legislator was necessary "to keep them all [the people] in awe." If law is often a powerful sword of autocracy, then custom may shield the people: "Custom, that unwritten law/By which the people keep even their kings in awe."[6] Some, like Chesterton, even argue that custom expands democracy by enfranchising the dead. But other theorists reject this comparison of custom to suffrage: they argue that we do not consent to our customs, as we do to our laws. If we strongly identify political liberty with deliberation and choice, then, says Bentham, the elected legislature is the true source of democratic legitimacy. And today, many jurists and political theorists see customary international law as a direct threat to democratic sovereignty: are we prepared to submit our own elected bodies to the rule of customary international law?

It is often claimed that custom, unlike law, is a static regime, even though spoken language always evolves more quickly than does written language. How are we to understand the evolution of custom? Some theorists argue

---

5. For Pindar, see Herodotus, *The Histories* 3.38. Chrysostom: "the laws create a polity of slaves, our customs, on the contrary, create a polity of free men." Chrysostom, "Discourse 76: Of Custom" Trans. H. Lamar Crosby in *Dio Chrysostom* Vol. 5 (Cambridge: Harvard University Press, 1951) 253 and 255.

6. Charles Davenant (1677), as quoted in Bederman, David J. *Custom as a Source of Law* (Cambridge: Cambridge University Press, 2010) 181.

that the growth of custom is purely adventitious, but others argue that custom, like common law, "works itself pure." In this broadly Burkean view, custom evolves toward greater utility and economic efficiency: custom is winnowed by the fans of history so that what survives must be in some way advantageous to the community. By contrast, Bentham saw in legal custom largely the sinister interests of the legal profession.

Custom plays a variety of roles in any legal system. The customs of merchants or of statesmen can be a source of law; the customs of the court shape the interpretation and application of law; and the customs of the people or of legal officials can abolish law through desuetude. I will not attempt to provide a systematic or comprehensive theory of all the roles that custom plays in a legal system. I will offer, however, a new and general theoretical approach to the study of custom by analyzing the notion of custom into two more basic logical concepts: convention and habit. All customs represent the intersection of social conventions and individual habits: customs are always conventional habits and habitual conventions. Some habits are idiosyncratic and not customary while some conventions are not habitual. Instead of distinguishing the objective usage from the subjective attitudes of participants, I propose to distinguish the habitual (individual) dimension of custom from the conventional (social) dimension of custom. As we shall see, all major theorists of custom wrestle with understanding the relation between the conventional and the habitual dimensions of custom.

So the philosophy of customary law revolves around a small set of fundamental themes: the relation of objective usage and subjective attitudes in custom, whether people consent to their own customs, whether customs have democratic legitimacy, whether customs promote the common good, whether custom "works itself pure" over time, and whether custom controls law. Since these themes are richly illuminated in the thought of the great philosophers of customary law, I provide a careful exegesis of the thought of these major theorists, but my interest is not primarily exegetical but philosophical. I employ a method of philosophical reconstruction of these classic texts in which I begin with exegesis but then focus on a philosophical evaluation of the central claims. Engaging these major thinkers provokes a series of reflections on the nature and significance of custom and customary law.

In the first chapter, I explore the theory of social order in Aristotle. In response to the Sophists' familiar contrast of nature and convention, Aristotle distinguishes natural, customary, and stipulated social order. I show that Aristotle uses two different words for custom: *ethos* captures the habitual dimension of custom while *nomos* captures the conventional dimension. Drawing on contemporary philosophical analyses of habit and convention, I then argue that customs are habitual conventions and conventional habits. In the second chapter, we shall see Francisco Suárez develop his theory of custom and customary law in direct response to the views of Aristotle and Thomas Aquinas. As a voluntarist, Suárez argues that all law gets its authority from the will of the sovereign; yet custom seems to arise spontaneously. Suárez develops a set of sophisticated arguments that attempt to show that the people consent to their customs and that the prince tacitly consents to those customs he does not revoke. No philosopher explores the relationship between objective usage and subjective consent in custom with deeper insight than does Suárez. Here we explore the question of what it would mean to consent to custom and ask if people might have reasons to conform to custom without consenting to them. In the third chapter, I examine Jeremy Bentham's metaphysics of custom. More than any other philosopher, Bentham attempts to ground custom in ontology, epistemology, and linguistics—largely in direct opposition to Aristotle and Aquinas. We explore issues such as the following: Are customs an aggregate of habits or a logical whole? How can we discern a custom when we only observe individual habits? Do customs have any obligatory force before they are recognized by courts? Are customs compatible with democratic legitimacy?

In the fourth chapter, I turn to the leading American representative of the historical school of jurisprudence, James Coolidge Carter. Why Carter? Carter was perhaps the most important practicing American lawyer of the Gilded Age. Although not an academic jurist of the rank of Savigny or Maine, Carter both sums up the insights of the historical school and pioneers the rise of legal anthropology and legal sociology. Carter makes an insightful and provocative case for customary law on the grounds that custom is the mode of social order most compatible with individual liberty. The yoke of custom becomes a second nature or invisible constraint. Carter also shows effectively that many usages that are often regarded as bad customs are not customs at all. Finally, Carter helps us to see that the process of adjudication rests upon modes of tacit knowledge that cannot ever be codified. Although it is true that Carter is not a rigorous philosopher, I think we shall discover that his inconsistencies and mistakes are deeply illuminating. It is a melancholy truth that the most insightful thinkers are often not the most logically rigorous.

Aristotle, Suárez, Bentham, and Carter are an odd collection of legal theorists, but I know of no other theorists who devoted such sustained philosophical analysis to custom and customary law. Coke and Hale are great theorists of the common law; Savigny and Maine are great theorists of legal evolution: but about the general theory of custom these jurists offer only casual asides and scattered aperçus. Moreover, each of our chosen theorists directly responds to the claims of his predecessors, creating a lively and illuminating dialectic. Their arguments are not so much cumulative as complementary: each offers an insightful and original take on customary law. This book is something more than "four philosophies of customary law" but something less than a systematic "philosophy of customary law": it is a set of variations on some common themes. Moreover, I shall enrich my analysis of these classic theorists with discussions of many more contemporary theorists of custom and customary law.

This book grew out of an interdisciplinary and international conference on the nature of customary law that I organized with my colleague from Cambridge University, the late Amanda Perreau-Saussine de Ezcurra, held at Newnham College, Cambridge, on September 14–16, 2005. The papers from that conference were published in the book *The Nature of Customary Law: Legal, Historical, and Philosophical Perspectives*, edited by Amanda Perreau-Saussine and James Bernard Murphy (Cambridge: Cambridge University Press, 2007). My debt to Amanda, as a colleague and as a friend, is incalculable. This book is dedicated to her memory.

ACKNOWLEDGMENTS

While writing this book, I have benefited greatly from comments on each chapter by these scholars: Chapter One: Matthew Kramer and the other members of Kramer's seminar in legal theory at Cambridge. Chapter Two: Brian Tierney, John P. Doyle, and James Gordley. Chapter Three: Jerry Postema, Philip Schofield, and Mark S. Stein. Chapter Four: Lewis A. Grossman. I also wish to thank my tireless and talented research assistants and editors: Kirsten Murray, Lauren Rocco, Ji Hye Ha, Liz King, and Grace Park.

CHAPTER 1 | Habit and Convention at the Foundation of Custom

PHILOSOPHICAL JURISPRUDENCE—FROM PLATO to Hans Kelsen—rests upon three fundamental concepts of order and three allied concepts of law: the order intrinsic to human nature grounds the natural law, the order found in informal social practices grounds the customary law, and deliberately stipulated order grounds enacted law. As with many sets of foundational concepts, these are often defined or at least described in terms of each other.[1] This set of analogies and contrasts between nature, custom, and deliberate stipulation forms the deep structure of traditional philosophical jurisprudence: they are the conceptual lenses and tools by which philosophical analysis of law has proceeded. The history of philosophical jurisprudence reveals how rare it is to examine the lenses by which we see and the tools by which we dissect.[2]

---

1. This circle of concepts lives on in Pierre Bourdieu's recent description of custom (*habitus*) both as "immanent law" and as "history turned into nature." Pierre Bourdieu, *Outline of a Theory of Practice*, Trans. Richard Nice (Cambridge: Cambridge University Press, 1977) 78–81.

2. Theories of positive law, for example, oscillate unstably between two implicit contrasts, with natural law and with customary law. Positive law is said to lack the intrinsic moral force of natural law: Aquinas, for example, contrasts the natural law precept ("you shall not kill") with the positive law precept ("you shall not wear garments sewn from wool and linen together"). In relation to natural law, then, the theory of positive law is an account of the relation between morality and law: Does all law have some kind of moral force? Is there a moral obligation to obey the law? At the same time, however, positive law is also contrasted with customary law, in the sense that positive law is deliberately imposed or posited from above while customary law grows up from below. I analyze the structure of the discourse of positive law in Plato, Aquinas, Hobbes, and Austin in my book *The Philosophy of Positive Law: Foundations of Jurisprudence* (New Haven: Yale University Press, 2005).

Sometimes customary habits are compared to natural instincts because they operate spontaneously, automatically, and tacitly. Custom here means a kind of second nature: our customary habits operate as unobtrusively as our breathing. In this sense, custom is like natural instinct except that it is learned in a particular social context. Yet custom is also described as a set of informal conventions, a set of practices of social coordination that arise from informal agreements without being imposed by enacted law. Custom here is an unwritten law: customary conventions differ from enacted conventions only by not being deliberately stipulated or imposed.

Custom, in short, must be analyzed into two basic notions: habit and convention. Habit and convention are logically independent. Not all habits are customary habits: many habits are purely idiosyncratic and do not serve as coordinating conventions. Similarly, many conventions are not habits. Indeed, some conventions are designed never to become merely habitual, like the conventions defining what is fashionable or the conventions defining secret codes. Mathematicians and other special communities often adopt explicit conventions of notation, procedure, or protocol that, at least initially, are not habitual. Or, to use Hume's example, two rowers coordinating their strokes may do so by signal or by deliberate imitation without any element of habit. As we shall see, conventions over time often depend upon the formation of supportive habits, but not all conventions rest on habits. All customs are habitual conventions and conventional habits: custom naturalizes conventions just as it conventionalizes human nature. Clear thinking about custom will require us to distinguish the dimension of the habitual from the dimension of the conventional. I sketch such an analysis in this chapter.

Transcending the Nature-Convention Dichotomy[3]

The familiar dichotomy between nature and convention, or as we now say, nature and nurture, displaces the unique role of custom. The ancient Greek Sophists famously framed our analysis of human social institutions

---

[3] My discussion here and in the next section of the kinds of social order and the logic of social order, draws freely from my own work. See James B. Murphy, *The Moral Economy of Labor: Aristotelian Themes in Economic Theory* (New Haven: Yale University Press, 1993); and "Nature, Custom, and Reason in Aristotelian Political Science," in *The Review of Politics* 64 (Summer 2002) 469–495; and *The Philosophy of Positive Law: Foundations of Jurisprudence* (New Haven: Yale University Press, 2005).

in terms of a stark choice between what is natural and what is conventional.[4] Yet the greatest of the Sophists had already begun to transcend this stark dichotomy. Protagoras said, "Learning from teaching (*didaskalia*) requires both nature (*phusis*) and practice (*askēsis*)."[5] Plato also developed a version of this triad when he observed that "if you have a natural ability (*phusei*) for rhetoric, you will become a famous rhetorician, provided you supplement your ability with knowledge (*epistēmē*) and practice (*meletē*)."[6] Aristotle, in turn, agrees on the need for all three qualities: "Now some think that we become good by nature (*phusei*), others by habit (*ethei*), still others by teaching (*didakē*)."[7] Some Sophists argued that intellectual and moral excellences come from natural genius; others argued that these virtues come from deliberate teaching. But Protagoras, Plato, and Aristotle reframe the analysis. Rather than accept the choice between nature and convention, they insist on both. In this view, man is by nature a conventional animal and social conventions are how we actualize our natural potential.

The dichotomy between nature and convention obscures the crucial distinction between conventions that arise from tacit practice and conventions that are deliberately stipulated. True, we can assimilate custom to the notion of convention by distinguishing formal from informal conventions, but custom also refers to the tacit or intuitive dimension of social life. And we can assimilate customary habits to the notion of natural instincts, but then custom also refers to conventions. Therefore, it requires very Procrustean methods to force custom into the familiar dichotomy between nature and convention.

---

4. Throughout the fifth century, nomos and phusis were treated as antithetical. Some Sophists championed phusis (Antiphon, Callicles) while others championed nomos (Glaukon, Protagoras). See W.K.C. Guthrie, *History of Greek Philosophy*, Vol. 3 (Cambridge: Cambridge University Press, 1969) Chap. 4.

5. Protagoras in *Die Fragmente der Vorsokratiker*, Eds. Hermann Diels and Walter Kranz (Berlin: Weidmannsche Verlagsbuchhandlung, 1954), Frag. 3. Usually *didaskalia* is rendered as "teaching" but Paul Shorey is right to argue that "learning" fits the context better, since the focus is on the conditions that promote successful learning in the student, of which teaching is only one. Shorey traces the history of Protagoras's triadic conception of education through Plato and all the way to Cicero's *ingenii, exercitatio dicendi, ratio aliqua* (*Pro Archias*). See his "*Physis, Meletē, Epistēmē*" in *Transactions and Proceedings of the American Philological Association* 40 (1909): 185–201.

6. Plato, *Phaedrus* 269D. Greek text: Oxford Classical Texts, Ed. John Burnet (Oxford: Clarendon Press, 1901). All Plato translations from *Plato: Complete Works*, Ed. John Cooper (Indianapolis: Hackett, 1997).

7. Aristotle, *Nicomachean Ethics* (Hereafter NE), Greek Text: Oxford Classical Texts, Ed. L. Bywater (Oxford: Clarendon Press, 1894) 1179b 20. All Bekker numbers keyed to the Greek texts. To render certain technical terms consistently in English, I have sometimes altered the generally excellent translations in *The Complete Works of Aristotle*, Ed. Jonathan Barnes (Princeton: Princeton University Press, 1984).

Why attempt to transcend the Sophistic dichotomy? First, a human being apart from all cultural artifice would lack his very nature. The challenge is to understand how nature and culture interact both in the development of each individual person and in the development of human social and political life. Second, custom tends to naturalize our conventions by making them intuitive and automatic. Individuals acquire their intellectual and moral excellence both by tacit emulation and by explicit instruction; societies acquire their conventions both by tacit practices of social custom and by the deliberate institution of legislation. When conventions become habitual they evolve from being objects of analysis to modes of analysis: habitual conventions are not what we see but the means by which we see. That is why every society depends upon foreigners to describe its customs: we cannot see our own customs because we see with them.

Aristotle used this triadic logic of explanation more than any other ancient thinker. He says, for example, "in order to become good and wise requires three things; these are nature, habit, and reason (*phusis, ethos, logos*)."[8] Here Aristotle is speaking of the components of moral and intellectual self-realization: we must begin with the right natural capacities, we must cultivate these capacities into the right dispositions and habits of character, and we must use reason to reflectively adjust our habits in light of our ideals. In this model of self-realization, our habits presuppose our nature but cannot be reduced to it, just as our rational ideals presuppose our habits but cannot be reduced to them. Aristotle extended his triad beyond individual self-realization to the actualization of the political community. Thus, he says in many places (e.g., *Politics* 1332b 8–11), the legislator, in the deliberate stipulation of law, must take into account the natural capacities of his citizens as well as their social customs.

Although this triadic model of social explanation never achieved the ubiquity and familiarity of the Sophistic dichotomy, it appears frequently throughout the history of Western theories of language and of law. In the theory of language, we find John Poinsot (John of St. Thomas) asking "whether the division of signs in to natural (*naturale*), stipulated (*ad placitum*), and customary (*ex consuetudine*) is a sound division."[9] By natural signs he means those signs that relate to their objects independent of human activity: smoke is a sign of fire. By customary signs he means those signs that arise from the tacit social practices of human communities: napkins

---

8. Aristotle, *Politics*, Greek text: Oxford Classical Texts, Ed. W. D. Ross (Oxford: Clarendon Press, 1957) 1332a 38.

9. John Poinsot, *Tractatus de Signis* [1632], Ed. and Trans. John Deely (Berkeley: University of California Press, 1985) 269.

on a table are a sign that dinner is imminent. By stipulated signs he means those signs whose meaning is deliberately appointed by an individual, as when a new word is introduced.[10] In the history of jurisprudence, our triad appears in a variety of guises. The author of the *Rhetorica Ad Herennium* (II, 19) says that law (*ius*) can arise by nature (*natura*), by statute (*lege*), and by custom (*consuetudine*) as well as in other ways. The jurist Ulpian famously distinguishes natural law, the customary law of nations, and civil law (*Digest* 1.1.1).

Recently, Friedrich Hayek has argued that the nature-convention dichotomy embodies the assumption that all social order is either natural or deliberately instituted, thereby ignoring the crucial role of spontaneous order, such as we find in language, law, and the market. "Yet much of what we call culture is just such a spontaneously grown order [e.g. custom], which arose neither altogether independently of human action [nature] nor by design [stipulation], but by a process that stands between these two possibilities, which were long considered as exclusive alternatives."[11] Hayek traces his notion of spontaneous order to Adam Ferguson: "Nations stumble upon establishments, which are indeed the result of human action, but not the execution of any human design."[12] Hayek argues that the totalitarian disasters of the twentieth century all shared the hubris of attempting to impose a deliberately stipulated order on society without regard for the existing natural and customary social orders in place. In his view, these totalitarian projects were not just crimes, they were also mistakes—the mistake of thinking that natural and customary social order could be replaced by deliberately designed order.

If we are to understand custom, we must transcend the false dichotomy between nature and convention. Custom, Janus-like, faces toward human nature and toward stipulated law. Custom turns our natural propensities toward eating, competing, and mating into complex conventions of dining, gaming, and marrying; custom also turns our deliberate rational and legal conventions of arguing, evaluating, and judging into tacit practices as spontaneous and fluid as natural instinct. Custom transforms the raw material of our generic human nature into a second, culturally specific nature: for example, we are born with the potential to learn any natural

10. For a critique and reconstruction of Poinsot's doctrine of signs, see James B. Murphy, "Nature, Custom, and Stipulation in the Semiotic of John Poinsot," *Semiotica* 83 1/2 (1991): 33–68.

11. F. A. Hayek, "Kinds of Order in Society" [1964] in *The Politicization of Society*, Ed. Kenneth Templeton, Jr. (Indianapolis: Liberty Press, 1979) 509.

12. Adam Ferguson, *An Essay on the History of Civil Society* (Edinburgh: A. Millar and T. Caddel, 1767) 187.

language—a propensity that custom transforms into a particular natural language. It is revealing that we call the systems of highly artificial linguistic conventions "natural" languages. Our customary languages are natural in two senses: they arise from our innate propensities, are developed into very complex and artificial systems of sound and meaning; and then, through the mechanisms of habituation, they become as tacit, spontaneous, and fluid as natural instinct. In this way our innate natural linguistic capacities are conventionalized just as our artificial linguistic conventions are naturalized.

Custom is able to effect this double transformation because of the close psychological relation of habit formation and social convention. If our habits were not shaped by social convention and if our social conventions were not generally habituated, there would be a deep chasm between our natural propensities and our social conventions. Our spoken languages would feel as forced and artificial as Esperanto or Fortran; our social life as challenging and strange as Kabuki theater. We would have to choose between the easy but crude natural propensities to grunt or to feed and the very demanding but refined conventions of speaking and eating. To some extent, no doubt, each of us does feel torn between the attractions of simpler, more natural modes of expression and the elaborate refinements of social conventions. But custom greatly reduces the chasm between easy spontaneity and challenging social choreography. Through custom, a great deal of artifice in our manners and mores, the labor of centuries, has become easy, spontaneous, reflexive, and even pleasurable.

The Two Faces of Custom: Ethos

The two faces of custom are ethos and nomos. In Aristotle, both words can refer to custom, but each has a different semantic field. Ethos, as customary habit, faces toward nature and the subrational passions while nomos, as customary convention, faces toward law and reason. Ethos naturalizes our conventions into our second nature, while nomos conventionalizes our natural propensities into an unwritten law. Aristotle often uses the term *ethos* to describe, not just the customs of men, but also the habits of animals. In a passage describing the *scala naturae* quoted above, he says that some animals are influenced by ethos, while man alone has reason (*Pol.* 1332b 4). As we shall see, Aristotle closely links reason with nomos; he never says that animals are guided by nomos. In his treatise *History of Animals* (HA), Aristotle uses the word ethos to describe the behavior of animals: he says that sheep gather together "within the sheepfold because of their ethos" (HA 611a2).[13] More often he uses *ēthos*[14] to describe the distinctive character of animals: "Their activities and modes of living vary according to their characters (*ēthē*) and their food" (HA 588a 18). Just as animals are closer to nature and further from reason, so are children and barbarians. Thus Aristotle says that the young are guided more by character (*ēthos*) than by reason (*logos*), whereas the old are more guided by reason than by character (*Rhetoric* 1389a 33 and 1390a 16).[15] And he claims that "many barbarians have a custom (*ethos*) of plunging their children at birth into a cold stream.... For human nature should early be habituated (*ethizein*) to endure all which by habit (*ethizein*) it can be made to endure..." (*Pol.* 1336a 15ff).

The reason why the conduct of animals, children, and barbarians is regulated by ethos rather than by nomos is that they are all dominated by the nonrational soul. Aristotle famously says that moral virtue comes from habit, as evidenced by the fact that the word moral (*ēthikē*) comes from *ethos* (NE 1103a 16; *EE* 1220a 40). The moral virtues, he says, are perfections of the nonrational part of the soul while the intellectual virtues are perfections of the rational part of the soul (NE 1103a 4). For this reason, he says, the intellectual virtues stem from teaching while the moral virtues stem from habit (NE 1103a 16). By ethos, we educate our passions, appetites, and pleasures so that they harmonize with the demands of practical reason. Animals, children, and barbarians also have passions, appetites, and pleasure that should be habituated in accordance with practical reason, but in their cases, the reason that regulates their habits must come from an adult. Similarly, Aristotle strongly contrasts the mere handicraftsmen (*cheirotechnēs*) who work by habit (*ethos*) with the master craftsman (*architektōn*) who works by reason (*logos*). He even says that the handicraftsmen make things without knowing what they are making, just as fire burns (*Metaphysics* 981b 3). So ethos is more like nature than like reason.

That ethos looks to nature more than to reason is evident in Aristotle's doctrine that ethos becomes a second nature. Aristotle frequently emphasizes the continuity between our natural propensities and our acquired habits. Ethos is like nature because it is spontaneous, voluntary, and pleasant: "it must be pleasant to move toward a natural state of being.... Habits

---

13. Greek text: *Aristotle: Historia Animalium Vol. I: Books I–X: Text.* Ed. D. M. Balme (Cambridge: Cambridge University Press, 2002).

14. Aristotle tells us that *ēthos* comes from ethos at *Eudemian Ethics* 1220a 39. Greek text: Oxford Classical Texts, Ed. R. R. Walzer and J. M. Mingay (Oxford: Clarendon Press, 1991).

15. Greek text of *Rhetoric*: Oxford Classical Texts, Ed.W. D. Ross (Oxford: Oxford University Press, 1959).

(*ethē*) also are pleasant; for as soon as a thing has become habitual (*ethos*) it is virtually natural (*physei*)." By contrast, what is painful is what is forced on us "for force is contrary to nature (*para physin*)." In order to acquire a new skill, we must force ourselves to concentrate, strain, and apply effort, all of which, says Aristotle, is necessarily painful: "they all involve compulsion and force, unless we are accustomed (*ethisthōsin*) to them, in which case it is ethos that makes them pleasant" (*Rhetoric* 1369b 34ff). Once we have mastered a skill, however, it becomes both habitual and pleasant. Ethos is like nature because it creates a predictable pattern of events: "what happens often is akin to what happens always, natural events happen always and habitual events often" (*Rhetoric* 1370a 7). Ethos is like nature because it is difficult to change: "it is easier to change a habit (*ethos*) than to change one's nature; even habit is hard to change just because it is like nature" (NE 1152a 30). Ethos is like nature because it is automatic, reflexive, and rapid: "If, then, the mind has not moved in an old path, it tends to move to the more customary (*synētheia*); for custom (*ethos*) now assumes the role of nature. Hence the rapidity with which we recollect what we frequently think about. For as one thing follows another by nature (*physei*), so too that happens by custom (*synētheia*), and frequency creates nature" (*Memory* 452a 28).[16] Ethos is like nature, finally, because it plays such a large role in our lives: "in every one ethos is a matter of importance, since it soon becomes nature" (*Problems* 949a 28).[17] In short, Aristotle makes it clear that habit naturalizes our conventions to such an extent that our second nature becomes almost indistinguishable from our original nature; indeed, he even says that our second nature largely replaces our first.

The shortcoming of Aristotle's use of ethos to refer to both habit and custom is that he has no easy way to distinguish habit from custom. Not all habits are customary habits: many are purely idiosyncratic.[18] So Aristotle does not distinguish individual habits from social customs. Similarly, by using the word ethos to describe both the instincts of animals as well as the customs of men, Aristotle does not always distinguish the natural behavior of animals from the acculturation of men. He refers to an animal's or plant's species-specific behavior as its character (*ēthos*, HA 488b 12, 588a 18),

---

16. Greek text: G.R.T. Ross, *Aristotle: De Sensu and De Memoria* (Cambridge: Cambridge University Press, 1906).

17. Greek text: *Aristotle: Problems II*, Ed. W. S. Hett (Cambridge: Harvard University Press, 1937).

18. Aristotle's term for a stable disposition, *hexis*, is sometimes translated as "habit," but a *hexis* is an objective and unchanging disposition, not a subjective psychological habit that waxes and wanes. Aristotle calls science, art, wisdom, and the moral virtues "*hexeis*"; but a virtue is much more than a habit.

whereas we think of habits as what individuate us and of customs as what distinguish one society from another within the same species.

The Two Faces of Custom: Nomos

If ethos looked toward our passionate nature, then nomos looks toward our rational law. Aristotle frequently associates nomos with mind (*nous*) and with reason (*logos*). Although nomos refers broadly to conventions both legal and customary, the etymology of nomos always implied that the convention stemmed from an act of deliberate stipulation. According to Ostwald: "There is universal agreement, as far as I know, that this noun (*nomos*) is derived from the same root as *nemō*, whose basic concept involves a 'distribution' or 'assigning' of some kind."[19] To which W.K.C. Guthrie adds: "That is to say, it presupposes an acting subject—believer, practitioner or apportioner—a mind from which the nomos emanates."[20] This etymology helps us to understand Aristotle's strong identification of law with reason: "nomos has compulsive power, while it is at the same time a reason (*logos*) proceeding from a sort of practical wisdom (*phronēsis*) and mind (*nous*)" (NE 1180a 21). Aristotle says that for nomos to rule is for "God and mind alone to rule" because "nomos is mind without desire" (*Pol.* 1287a 29–32).[21] In short, we share ethos with other animals while we share nomos with God.

Aristotle develops not only a rationalist account of law but also a legalist conception of reason. Virtue, he says, means not only to act in accordance with reason (*kata logon*) but to act by means of reason (*meta logou*): "It implies that the agent is conscious of the rule he follows, that he acts not merely 'by rule' but 'with a rule'."[22] To act according to reason is thus to act according to an external standard, such as law (*kata nomon*). According to Aristotle, logos is like a lawgiver, since logos commands, orders, and defends.[23] Nomos and logos are so closely linked that in some places the

---

19. Ostwald, *Nomos and the Beginnings of the Athenian Democracy* (Oxford: Clarendon Press, 1969) 9.
20. Guthrie, *History of Greek Philosophy*, Vol. 3, 55.
21. Since Aristotle says that law proceeds from practical wisdom *phronēsis*, he cannot literally mean that law is reason without desire. Practical wisdom is rational desire and a desiring reason. "For Aristotle moral action was reason penetrated by desire, and law was the handmaid of morality: it existed to habituate men to virtue. Law must therefore share the appetitive and purposive element which is found in virtue itself." Francis Wormuth, "Aristotle on Law," in his *Essays in Law and Politics* Ed. Dalmas H. Nelson and Richard L. Sklar (Port Washington, NY: Kennikat Press, 1978) 14–26, at 17.
22. John Burnet's gloss on NE 1144b 25 in his *The Ethics of Aristotle* (London: Methuen 1900) 37.
23. NE, 1114b 29; 1115b 19; 1117a 8; 1119a 20, 1125b 35; 1138b 20. On logos as nomos, see Gauthier, René and Jean Jolif, *L'Ethique à Nicomaque*. Vol. 2 (Louvain: Publications Universitaires, 1970) 149.

Aristotelian manuscripts vary and scholars cannot agree on which is correct: for example, "this is why we do not allow a man to rule, but nomos (or logos)."[24] Since Aristotle often treats these words as synonyms, either makes perfect sense.

As applied to custom, Aristotle's close identification of nomos and logos seems odd. We can see how statutes might embody deliberate stipulation, but what about custom? Customs seem to arise from human conduct but not from any deliberate design. Perhaps Aristotle uses nomos to refer only to statute and not to custom? Unfortunately, there are a number of passages in which nomos refers broadly to convention, both customary and legal. Whenever he adopts the Sophistic contrast of nature and convention (nomos), he is using nomos broadly to include customs and laws. First, when he contrasts natural justice to conventional justice (*dikaion nomikon*), he is using nomos to refer broadly to conventions, including weights and measures, which are often informal. He says that these kinds of conventional justice—which would include both customs and statues—are just by agreement (*kata synthēkēn*) (NE 1134b 18 and 35). Second, when he contrasts slavery according to nature with slavery according to convention, he means nomos to include custom since he illustrates conventional slavery in reference to the custom that "whatever is taken in war belongs to the victors"—a convention that clearly was not statutory (*Pol.* 1255a 5). Third, Aristotle says that money (*nomisma*) "exists not by nature but by nomos" (NE 1133a 29) because money rests upon an agreement (*kata synthēkēn*). Is Aristotle claiming that all money is legal tender stemming from enactment? Or does not money also arise from customary agreements about a medium of exchange?

I think it clear that in these contrasts of nature and nomos, Aristotle means nomos to include conventions broadly, both customary and legal. When Aristotle wishes to emphasize the customary and informal character of conventions, he uses variants of nomos, such as *nomima* and forms of the verb *nomizō*. By contrast, when Aristotle wishes to emphasize the statutory character of conventions, he modifies nomos with variants of the verb *tithēmi*, to lay down: a statute, then, is a convention that is imposed or "laid down."

Aristotle also compares legal to customary conventions when he contrasts written to unwritten law (*nomos agraphos*). He says that a legislator "should provide enacted laws (*nomoi*) both written and unwritten" (*Pol.* 1319b 40). It is not clear how a legislator can enact customs, but Aristotle

---

24. NE 1134a 35. Gauthier and Jolif favor nomos but Bywater favors logos.

wants legislators to be concerned with both fostering customs and laying down laws. He does, however, make it quite clear that the unwritten law is custom when he says that "customs (*ethē*) have more authority and concern more important matters than do written laws" (*Pol.* 1287b 5). Aristotle does not explain here why custom is more authoritative and concerns more important matters than written law. Perhaps custom is more authoritative because it rests upon ancient and widely shared norms while written laws often rest merely upon transient partisan regimes. And perhaps the very weighty matters of family life and divine worship are largely regulated by custom. In the *Rhetoric* (1375a 16), Aristotle points to another advantage of custom: "written laws depend on force while unwritten laws (*dikaia agrapha*) do not." Here Aristotle is referring to the habitual dimension of custom: because habits create a second nature, we do what custom demands spontaneously, without coercion.

Sometimes Aristotle contrasts written and unwritten law, not as statute and custom, but as local law and universal law. "Law (*nomos*) is either special (*idios*) or universal (*koinos*). By special law I mean that written law which regulates the life of a particular community; by universal law, all those unwritten things which are supposed to be acknowledged everywhere" (*Rhetoric* 1368b 7). Aristotle illustrates some of the principles of the universal unwritten law: "gratitude to, or requital of, our benefactors, readiness to help our friends, and the like" (*Rhetoric* 1374a 24). Some customs, in other words, are purely local conventions while others are universal norms: "Universal law is the law of nature (*kata physin*). For there really is, as everyone to some extent divines, a natural justice and injustice that is common to all, even to those who have no association or agreement with each other" (*Rhetoric* 1373b 6). Commentators vary in their assessments of the transformation of unwritten law from local custom into the law of nature. Rudolf Hirzel sees only a nominal change: "*Die Sache bleibt, die Namen wechseln.*" But Francis Wormuth sees "an astonishing evolution."[25] Aristotle is moving rapidly around his circle of interdefinability: custom is both second nature and unwritten law—and universal unwritten law is the law of nature.

If ethos created ambiguities by sometimes blurring the important distinction between idiosyncratic and social habits, nomos creates some

25. Wormuth, "Aristotle on Law," 21. But Wormuth goes on to say (23) that we ought not to build an Aristotelian jurisprudence on the basis of a few sentences in the *Rhetoric*: "We are not obliged to believe that the *Rhetoric* is doing anything more than reporting the stock phrases of current oratory; and indeed the huddling together of unwritten law, universal law, natural justice, and equity is unlike the careful analysis Aristotle bestows on ideas he takes seriously."

ambiguities between customary and legal conventions. We saw that Aristotle says that money (*nomisma*) exists, not by nature, but by nomos. Does he mean that money arises from customary usage or from legal enactment? According to Eric Roll, the medieval scholastics translated Aristotle's nomos as *lex*, leading them to confuse legal tender money with money as a medium of exchange created by usage.[26]

In some places, it is genuinely difficult to decide whether Aristotle is referring to custom or to law. He says that "nomos does not command a man to kill himself, and what it does not command, it forbids" (NE 1138a 6).[27] Some commentators claim that Aristotle here means that "law does not expressly permit suicide, and whatever killing is not expressly permitted must be assumed to be forbidden."[28] Although this might be a plausible interpretation of the law of killing, Aristotle's claim is much broader. J. A. Stewart argues that Aristotle's claim is much more plausible if we think of him as referring to custom rather than to law: "Custom or fashion does not tell Oxford undergraduates to go down to the River in academic dress; it therefore forbids them to do it. Nor do the Statutes of the University tell them; but the Statutes do not therefore forbid them. The Statutes are neutral in this matter, as in many others in which fashion takes a side."[29] Even Stewart's example is awkward: it would be more natural to say that custom requires that one wear nonacademic dress when going down to the River; by requiring nonacademic dress, custom implicitly forbids academic dress.

The Roles of Habit and Convention in Custom

Clear thought about custom is impossible unless, following Aristotle, we analyze custom into the two more primitive notions of habit and convention. What is the relation between habit and convention in custom? Conventions serve both to create and to coordinate complex arenas of human activity.[30]

---

26. Eric Roll, *A History of Economic Thought* (Englewood Cliffs, NJ: Prentice-Hall, 1956) 34.

27. Gauthier and Jolif comment: "Cette assertion surprenante a reçu un assez bon nombre d'explications." *L'Ethique à Nicomaque,* Vol. 2, 423.

28. See John Burnet, *The Ethics of Aristotle* 244. Max Hamburger follows Burnet and claims that Aristotle's text here "seems to be somewhat corrupt." *Morals and the Law* (New Haven: Yale University Press, 1951) 80.

29. J. A. Stewart, *Notes on the Nicomachean Ethics of Aristotle*, Vol. 1 (Oxford: Clarendon Press, 1982) 390.

30. David Lewis defines all conventions as solutions to coordination problems, but I accept Andrei Marmor's argument that some conventions are constitutive and not merely coordinating of activities. I discuss Lewis and Marmor below.

Conventions coordinate our activities much more effectively when they become habitual. If the conventional shapes and sounds of words were not grasped automatically by habit, then communication would grind to a halt, like a millipede trying to move each foot by explicit decision. Conversely, if habits were not conventional, we would be reduced to very diverse and idiosyncratic grunts, gestures, and actions, without any means of harmonizing mutual expectations of conduct. Either way, human social life as we know it would not be possible.

Habit gives convention motivational power and performative skill: habitual conventions have spontaneity, speed, and efficiency; they are usually pleasant, familiar, and easy. Conventions give habits cultural sophistication and a social life: conventional habits are often refined, elegant, meaningful, and shared; they enable us to know what to expect in the behavior of others, enable us to conform to others' expectations, and provide common criteria for evaluating our own and others' conduct. Of course, the marriage of habit and convention is not always a happy one: habitual conventions are often rigid, mechanical, blind, and stupid—think of the customary habits defining honor, insult, and duels. We often fail to reflect upon or critically challenge our habits and even were we to decide to change them, our old habits interfere with learning new ones, as we Americans discover in trying to speak a foreign language, or to drive in England. Similarly, conventionalized habits are often fussy, extravagant, superfluous, and silly—think of the customary conventions governing early modern court life. Conventions can become so artificial and elaborate that they smother the activities they are meant to foster and coordinate, like overly burdensome legal procedures. Nonetheless, as a broad generalization, we might say that conventions without habits are a burden while habits without conventions are a bore.

Habits bridge nature and culture just as conventions bridge custom and law. Habits do not arise from nothing; they are grafted onto our instinctive impulses.[31] Habits adapt our instincts to the particular conventions of our milieu: the instinct to eat or drink is modified by habit into the most astonishing diversity of dining conventions. The capacity to acquire and to regulate habits in normatively successful performances is called intelligence. Habits are best understood as a propensity for acquiring automatic routines. Psychologists often contrast controlled with automatic propensities: we might deliberately choose to initiate an automatic routine but

---

31. On the relation of habit to instinct, see James L. Mursell, "The Ontogenetic Significance of Instinct, Habit, and Intelligence" in *The Psychological Review* 29 (3) May 1922: 163–179.

we do not choose every step of it.[32] Automatic propensities include natural ones, like breathing and blinking; and learned ones, like stopping a car at a red light or speaking our native tongue. Habits are learned automatic propensities: breathing can be a habit since we can learn to change the instinctive pattern of our breathing. Sometimes we can deliberately interrupt and override our automated habits, as when we choose to run a red light; but sometimes we lose voluntary control over our habits, as when we would prefer not to grasp the meaning of a familiar spoken or written word. What a word signifies to us is not something we can directly control, which is why Chesterton famously said of the lights in Times Square: "how beautiful it would be to someone who could not read…" The process whereby a routine becomes automatic is itself automatic: we can partly shape this process by mnemonic strategies, but consciousness of our routines inexorably recedes over time.[33]

Habits are necessary because of our severely limited capacity for short-term memory: we could not respond in thought, feeling, or action to real-time events unless a good deal of our knowledge and skill were available in largely automatic routines.[34] We use our very limited conscious attention to learn, to activate, to monitor, and to revise these myriad automatic routines. Our concepts, attitudes, and stereotypes are habits of thought that enable us to process a large amount of information quickly but with considerable rigidity and overgeneralization. Habits organize knowledge and know-how into nested hierarchies, like Russian dolls or Chinese boxes. Every habitual routine, such as driving a car, actually involves many distinct subroutines, like starting or stopping the car.[35] By organizing our knowledge into discrete "chunks" or subroutines, we are able to handle a great deal of complex information by focusing only on the few larger bundles. Thus, although we can hold only a few random digits in our minds, we can memorize thousands of numbers by chunking them into meaningful bundles, such as phone numbers or batting averages.

---

32. For a comprehensive analysis of the literature on automaticity, see Agnes Moors and Jan De Houwer "Automaticity: A Theoretical and Conceptual Analysis" in *Psychological Bulletin* 132 (2) 2006: 297–326.

33. John A. Bargh and Tanya Chartrand, "The Unbearable Automaticity of Being," *American Psychologist* 54/7 (July 1999): 462–479 at 469.

34. On the modern psychology of automatic habits, see John A. Bargh, "Automaticity in Social Psychology," *Social Psychology: Handbook of Basic Principles* (New York: Guilford) 169–183.

35. "…the overarching goal to drive a car may give rise to several subsidiary acts, such as changing gears and turning the wheel. These subsidiary acts are goal-directed… [but] unintentional." Moors and De Houwer, "Automaticity: A Theoretical and Conceptual Analysis," 303.

By means of these hierarchies of routines and subroutines, we enjoy the immense advantages of habits, namely, cognitive economy and performance efficiency. Habits enable us to attain a Walter Mitty-ish detachment from our daily activities so that we can focus our attention on a few important decisions or just daydream.[36] Attention is a scarce cognitive resource: habits enable us to make the best use of it. Creating automatic routines also helps to ensure the reliability of our performances by partially insulating them from the distraction of thought or of new circumstances. But this very insularity of habit from deliberate thought and new circumstances can have many disadvantages: habitual stereotypes, for example, have been shown to resist change however adaptive or desirable.[37] Thus, we Americans feel impelled to speak English while in France and to drive on the right in England. We pay an undeniable price in rigidity and overgeneralization for the economy and efficiency of our habits. It is precisely this inertia and resistance to change that makes habit what William James called "the enormous flywheel of society, its most precious conservative agent."[38]

Deliberate conscious cogitation may be the highest and most noble activity of human beings, but it is hopelessly slow, awkward, and inadequate for the complexity of knowing and doing. We could accomplish almost nothing unless most of our knowledge and skill was habituated into automatic routines. Deliberate thought must be reserved for the learning, the initiation, the monitoring, and the revision of existing habits in light of new circumstances and ideals.[39] Alfred North Whitehead observed that we often hear that we need less habit and more critical reason. To the contrary, says Whitehead: "Civilisation advances by extending the number of important operations which we can perform without thinking about them. Operations of thought are like cavalry charges in a battle—they are strictly limited in number, they require fresh horses, and must only be made at the

---

36. See Wendy Wood et al. "Habits in Everyday Life: Thought, Emotion, and Action" in *Journal of Personality and Social Psychology* 83 (6) 2002: 1281–1297.

37. On the disturbing effects of habitual racial stereotypes on social behavior, see John A. Bargh et al. "Automaticity of Social Behavior: Direct Effects of Trait Construct and Stereotype Activation on Action" in *Journal of Personality and Social Psychology* 71 (2) 1996: 230–244.

38. James, *Principles of Psychology.* Vol. 1 (Cambridge: Harvard University Press, 1981) 125.

39. "To consciously and willfully regulate one's own behavior, evaluations, desires, and emotional states requires considerable effort and is relatively slow. Moreover, it appears to require a limited resource that is quickly used up, so conscious self-regulatory acts can only occur sparingly and for a short time.... the unconscious or automatic processes we've described here are unintended, effortless, very fast, and many of them can operate at any given time." Bargh and Tanya Chartrand, "The Unbearable Automaticity of Being," 476.

decisive moments."[40] Instead of less habit and more reason we need more rational habits.

By distinguishing habits from conventions we can understand how fashion relates to custom. The conventions defining what is fashionable seem much like other customs: they arise informally, are socially shared, and are enforced by ostracism. Yet fashion seems decidedly unlike custom in that fashions change so rapidly, while other customs evolve only gradually. There may well be a custom among certain groups to dress and live fashionably, but the content of the latest fashion is a good example of a convention that has not become habitual. Indeed, the point of fashion seems to be the fun of escaping the tyranny of old sartorial habits—though perhaps by erecting a new tyranny of up-to-date conformism.[41]

The modern philosophical analysis of conventions began with David Lewis's classic 1969 book, *Convention.* Lewis's basic analysis has been widely accepted but usefully revised recently by Andrei Marmor.[42] By looking briefly at Lewis and his critics, we shall see that although Lewis is focused on informal conventions, his account of those conventions relies too heavily on elements of knowledge, consent, and awareness typical of formal conventions. Lewis has neglected the role of habit in securing the concordant expectations that are the basis of social conventions. As we shall see, Lewis and Marmor have very different views of the relation of informal conventions to formal conventions. This debate will illuminate our understanding of the relationship of custom to law. Lewis's basic definition of convention, to which he adds several refinements, is this: "A regularity *R* in the behavior of members of a population *P* when they are agents in a recurrent situation *S* is a *convention* if and only if, in any instance of *S* among members of *P*, 1) everyone conforms to *R*; 2) everyone expects everyone else to conform to *R*; 3) everyone prefers to conform to *R* on condition that the others do, since *S* is a coordination problem and uniform conformity to *R* is a coordination equilibrium in *S*."[43] The basic idea here is one of a conditional preference: we prefer to conform to a convention just if everyone else conforms. According to Lewis, all conventions are solutions to coordination problems: if our phone conversation is disconnected, then

---

40. Whitehead, *Introduction to Mathematics* (New York: Holt, 1911) 61.

41. Matt Kramer pointed out this irony.

42. "David Lewis provided an ingenious account of social conventions that, at least in its core, has been widely accepted ever since." Andre Marmor, *Social Conventions* (Princeton: Princeton University Press, 2009) 19.

43. David K. Lewis, *Convention: A Philosophical Study* (Oxford: Blackwell, 2002) 42. cf. the final definition at 78.

we need a convention to determine which party should call back. We can't both successfully call back. We do not care whether the person who placed the call or the recipient makes the return call, so long as we agree who is responsible: "We may achieve coordination by acting on our concordant expectations about each other's actions."[44] Andrei Marmor rightly argues, however, that conventions do not merely regulate ongoing activities, such as driving; conventions also constitute new activities, such as chess.[45]

What matters most is that we agree, not what we agree about. In Justice Brandeis's description of legal conventions, "what matters is that that law is settled, not that it is settled right." As Andrei Marmor rightly observes about Lewis, we need not be indifferent to the content of a particular convention; we just need to prefer the existing rule to having no convention at all.[46] Wearing a raincoat in the rain is not a convention, on Lewis's account, if I prefer to avoid getting wet no matter what others do; nonetheless, wearing a raincoat might be a convention, if I prefer a raincoat to carrying an umbrella on the condition that I expect everyone else to wear a raincoat and I want to fit in.

We should note the logical structure of Lewis's account: conventions are explained by reference to our knowledge (of what others do) and our preferences (to belong to a group). Indeed, on Lewis's account, we must have knowledge not only of what people actually do but also of what they might do. Since preferences are inherently comparative, we must know that our preferred convention is but one of several possible coordination solutions: "there is no such thing as the only possible convention. . . . Any convention is arbitrary because there is an alternative regularity that could have been our convention instead."[47] According to Lewis, conventions must not only be arbitrary, their arbitrariness must be "common knowledge."[48]

Critics of Lewis have objected that these conditions of knowledge are not necessary for the existence of many conventions. Tyler Burge imagines an isolated tribe that thinks its own language is natural; he concludes that "participants in a conventional regularity need not know it is arbitrary."[49] Richard Grandy agrees with Burge and considers the example of Newspeak, a conventional language spoken in Orwell's *1984*: here, speakers strongly prefer not to speak Newspeak but do so purely out of

---

44. Lewis, *Convention* 27.
45. See Marmor, *Social Conventions* Chap. 2.
46. Andrei Marmor, *Positive Law and Objective Values* (Oxford; New York: Clarendon, 2001) 11.
47. Lewis, *Convention* 70.
48. Lewis, *Convention* 68.
49. Burge "On Knowledge and Convention" in *Philosophical Review* 84 (1975): 249–255 at 250.

fear. In anticipation of, and in response to, the criticism that people often don't have the knowledge of conditional preferences and of the alternatives they imply, Lewis weakens his knowledge conditions substantially, saying that this knowledge may be merely potential knowledge and "irremediably nonverbal knowledge."[50] Moreover, "when children and the feeble-minded conform to our conventions, they may not take part in them *as* conventions, for they lack any conditional preference for conformity to an alternative."[51] But with respect to many conventions, all of us may be childish and feeble-minded.[52]

Dale Jamieson does not analyze the structure of Lewis's arguments nor offer an alternative account of conventions, but he offers what he takes to be counterexamples of conventions that do not meet Lewis's criteria: his examples and Lewis's replies illuminate the role of habits in conventions. Jamieson argues that the convention of eating soup with a spoon arises simply out of unthinking habit: we do it because it does not occur to us to eat soup any other way and not because we expect others to do the same. Lewis replies that habit is not an alternative to convention, but is rather the product of convention: "We use the spoon by habit, and we use the spoon because we expect others to use spoons and we prefer to eat soup as others do. It is only because of the preference and expectation that the habit persists and succeeds in governing our unthinking use of the spoon. If ever I expected others to pour soup into their mouths through funnels, or if ever I preferred to be different, alternatives would at once occur to me and probably I would manage to overcome force of habit."[53]

Both Jamieson and Lewis incorrectly describe the role of habit in social conventions. Jamieson's "unthinking habit" does not distinguish idiosyncratic habits from conventional habits. I might well have a private habit for eating soup, but in public I am likely to adopt conventional habits, unless I have an unusual desire to be different. But Lewis does not see habitual imitation as the most common basis for the concordant expectations that are the basis of social conventions. Lewis treats the choice of whether to eat soup with a spoon or not as governing our habit: if we prefer to conform, we develop the habit of eating with a spoon but if we

---

50. Grandy, review of "Convention: A Philosophical Study," *The Journal of Philosophy* 74 (2) Feb. 1977: 63, 129–139 at 133.

51. Lewis, "Convention: Reply to Jamieson" in *Papers in ethics and social philosophy* (Cambridge: Cambridge University Press, 2000) 143; Lewis, *Convention* 75.

52. "People can simply be mistaken about the conventional nature of the rules they follow." Marmor, *Social Conventions* 6.

53. Dale Jamieson, "David Lewis on Convention," in *Canadian Journal of Philosophy*. Vol. 5, No. 1 (Sep., 1975) 75 and Lewis "Convention: Reply to Jamieson," 138.

prefer nonconformity we develop a different habit. Lewis does not see that we have a habitual propensity to imitate the behavior of those around us antecedent to any expectations we might have about how others behave or desires we might have to conform or not. There is a long tradition of psychological research showing that we have an automatic propensity to conform to the posture and behavior of those with whom we interact. These studies show that we mimic the behavior of others without being aware of doing so.[54] Although Lewis is right that we can override this automatic propensity to some extent by deliberately seeking nonconformity, conformity is not a choice so much as an automatic habit.

Let's take Lewis's use of Hume's example of two rowers in a single boat who coordinate their efforts without any explicit agreement: "We are always choosing whether to row faster or slower; it matters little to either of us at what rate we row, provided we row in rhythm. So each is constantly adjusting his rate to match the rate he expects the other to maintain."[55] Lewis's rowers are doing a lot of thinking, expecting, and deciding about how to coordinate their efforts. But, lucky for us, none of this is necessary because each rower has a habitual and automatic propensity to mimic the strokes of the other rower.[56] True, one rower could be willfully perverse and frustrate this natural harmony, but ordinarily habit, not thought, secures this very simple coordination. This automatic propensity to imitate helps to explain why precedent is the most common basis for conventional rules.

Why does Lewis place so much emphasis on the knowledge, preferences, and choices of the participants to social conventions? According to Burge, Lewis's whole analysis of conventions is guided by the central case of explicit formal agreements in which we do have knowledge of alternatives and an independent desire to coordinate our activities. Lewis's conventions are still not fully emancipated from the picture of a rational and knowledgeable deliberative body reaching an agreement. "But his account still takes too little note of the unconscious element in many conventions—and the possibility of their being essentially misconceived or misvalued."[57] In the case of formal conventions, that is, agreements, we

---

54. "There is a long history of research that suggests that perceptions of the behavior of one's interaction partner leads directly to tendencies to behave that way oneself. . . . No one had any awareness of engaging in these behaviors when asked at the end of the experiment." Bargh and Chartrand, "The Unbearable Automaticity of Being," 467.

55. Lewis, *Convention* 6.

56. "In a chameleon-like way, the participants' behavior automatically changed as a function of their social environment; as the behavior of their interaction partner changed, so did their own behavior." Bargh and Chartrand, "The Unbearable Automaticity of Being," 467.

57. Burge, "On Knowledge and Convention," 254–255. Marmor concurs with Burge in *Social Conventions* 6.

can safely assume that the participants treat them instrumentally: we come to agreements in order to secure our desires. But our tacit conventions of making or avoiding eye contact, of etiquette generally, and of language are not merely instruments we adopt to pursue our desires; these informal conventions shape our beliefs and desires. Customary conventions are often not adopted as rational strategies; rather we become accustomed to them, meaning that through the natural mechanisms of imitation and habit the particular conventions of our milieu shape who we are. Long before we can chose to adopt a convention we are already accustomed to a wide range of conventions. Because Lewis implicitly uses formal conventions as his model for all conventions, he neglects the habitual dimension of many informal conventions. He thus neglects the ways in which customary conventions become an invisible second nature and why we often depend upon foreigners to describe them to us.

What is the relationship of social conventions to legal conventions and other agreements? According to Marmor, Lewis's account of conventions excludes all formal agreements: "Conventions, in other words, emerge as solutions to recurrent coordination problems, not as a result of an agreement, but as an alternative to such an agreement, precisely in those cases where agreements are difficult or impossible to attain."[58] Yet, Lewis claims to offer a philosophical analysis of convention "in its full generality, including tacit convention not created by agreement."[59] Lewis thus proposes an account that includes both tacit conventions and deliberate agreements. Sometimes Lewis treats agreements as one species of convention: "Coordination by means of an agreement is not, of course, an alternative to coordination by means of concordant mutual expectations. Rather, agreement is one means of producing those expectations." Indeed, Lewis points out that agreements are such a good method of securing coordination, that we describe alternative methods as "tacit agreements." And, as we have seen, Lewis's own account of such tacit agreements draws on elements of knowledge, choice, and consent that we associate with formal agreements.[60]

Lewis does not say much about formal agreements, but he seems aware that sometimes they create reasons for acting that are not conventional. I might conform to an agreement purely to honor a promise, quite apart

---

58. Marmor, *Positive Law and Objective Values* 7. "As David Lewis was right to observe, conventions typically emerge as an alternative to agreements, precisely in those cases where agreements are difficult to obtain because of the large number of agents involved." *Social Conventions* 4.

59. Lewis, *Convention* 3.

60. Lewis, *Convention* 34–35.

from my expectations of what others will do; or I might conform to a law or treaty purely from fear of the sanction, again quite apart from any expectations I have about the behavior of others. Yet, even here, Lewis argues that these legal conventions are likely to evolve into social conventions, once the force of the original promises fades over time. Lewis says that it is "badly misleading" to say that we conform to many legal or constitutional conventions "because we once agreed to." Over time, he says, we forget the original agreement: "Then a convention erected by agreement is no longer different from one created otherwise: it bears no trace of its origin."[61]

What about legal sanctions? Don't they necessarily create independent reasons for acting quite apart from how others act? Using the example of the rules of the road, Lewis argues that legal sanctions are insignificant compared to the conventional reasons we have for conforming: "my preference for driving on the same side [of the road] as the others outweighs any incentive the highway patrol may give me to drive on the right." Lewis makes a general claim that disparages the importance of legal sanctions in enforcing social conventions: "The punishments are superfluous if they agree with our convention, are outweighed if they go against it, are not decisive either way, and hence to not make it any less conventional to drive on the right."[62] In short, Lewis wants to minimize the contrast between legal and social conventions by arguing either that legal conventions can evolve into social conventions or that social conventions remain conventions even when enacted into law.

Marmor, by contrast, excludes all legal enactments from his notion of conventions. For him, the Geneva Conventions are not conventions. He terms all such formal enactments "institutionalized practices" as opposed to conventions: "if legislative codification of conventions succeeds, the practice is no longer conventional."[63] The first difference between institutional practices (including law) and social conventions, he says, is that institutional practices include secondary rules that specify how the primary rules are created, revoked, or modified. By contrast, he says, conventions "are not enacted, they evolve gradually over time."[64] It is true that social conventions lack secondary rules but formal enactments also evolve gradually over time independently of those secondary rules. American constitutional law has evolved significantly quite apart from the formal amendment process, just as common law rules evolve quite apart from any

---

61. Lewis, *Convention* 84.
62. Lewis, *Convention* 44–45.
63. Marmor, *Social Conventions* 50.
64. Marmor, *Social Conventions* 51–52.

formal process of overruling precedents. In practice, then, the interpretation and application of law evolves in ways quite similar to the evolution of social conventions.

Marmor also points to the difference between formal legal sanctions and the informal sanctions of social conventions. He says that the absence of formal sanctions is what enables social conventions to evolve: because deviations from social conventions are permitted, they successively lead to new conventions. But Marmor offers no arguments or evidence to suggest that legal sanctions are more effective than informal sanctions, weakening his hypothesis about the effect of sanctions on the evolution of conventions. Consider the case of the convention of speaking English in the United States: were English made the official language, it would have virtually no effect on the use of English; indeed, were Spanish made the official language, that law would also have virtually no effect on the use of English. For many conventions, law seems superfluous. The French Academy has attempted to institutionalize the rules of French, complete with a set of sanctions, but this has not stopped the evolution of French. Whether and to what extent conventions evolve over time seems to have little to do with whether they are institutionalized or not.

Marmor often illustrates social conventions with the example of the rules of chess. Yet, he concedes that the rules of chess have been codified and institutionalized since 1929. So, are the rules of chess no longer conventions? Here Marmor makes an interesting distinction between professionals and amateurs: he claims that for tournament chess players, the rules are not conventions but for amateurs they are conventions.[65] Presumably, this is because professionals alone are likely to be aware of the institutional rules and motivated to avoid the official sanctions. Marmor does not extend this analysis to law, but one wonders whether many legal rules could be described as institutionalized for legal professionals but remain merely conventional for ordinary citizens? Marmor is committed to a basically lawyerly distinction among the sources of rules: any particular rule is either enacted or conventional. Lewis, by contrast, focuses on how norms function in practical reasoning: he sees no reason why a rule cannot begin as a law and then also become a convention or why a convention cannot remain a convention after it is enacted. In jurisprudential terms, this is the issue about whether a custom remains a custom after it is enacted and whether laws can become customary over time. Are law and custom mutually exclusive or can a rule be both lawful and customary?

---

65. Marmor, *Social Conventions* 51.

CHAPTER 2 | Customary Law in Suárez: Will of the Sovereign or of the People?

BECAUSE CUSTOMS ARE NOT in general deliberately made, customary law has always been the most profound challenge to any conception of law as the product of deliberate human stipulation. A close look at how Suárez attempts to square custom with his imperative theory of law will be deeply illuminating of the insights and blindness of any voluntarist approach to law. The deep quandaries produced by the attempt to account for customary law in terms of the will and reason of a lawgiver show no signs of abating. Ever since the ancient Roman jurists described custom as the tacit will of the people and the indirect command of the sovereign, lawyers and philosophers have attempted to interpret custom as an act of communication expressing either the consent of the people or the will of the sovereign. Even today, prominent legal philosopher Andrei Marmor insists that all law, including customary law, somehow expresses the will and approval of the sovereign.[1] To see how little has changed in the traditional doctrine that custom expresses the will of the people, compare the ancient Roman jurist Julian's famous quip that "what does it matter whether a

---

1. Marmor seems to reject the traditional view of custom: "Nor do I believe that Austin's device of 'tacit orders' can be salvaged from Hart's criticisms." But on the same page he then proceeds to affirm that traditional doctrine: "none of Hart's arguments can be taken to repudiate the idea that the law [including customary law] is basically a product of communication; it must be the product of an authority that expresses its views on the desirable behaviour of its alleged subjects…" It should be clear that Marmor has merely redescribed the traditional doctrine that custom expresses the tacit or indirect will of the sovereign. See Marmor, *Positive Law and Objective Values* (Oxford: Clarendon Press, 2001) 110.

people expresses its will by voting or by the substance of its actions?" with Marmor's much less felicitous endorsement of the same doctrine: "it seems to me that custom may well be regarded as an informal structure of a collective expression that is, in certain important respects, equivalent to the formal structures of collective decision-making, such as majority vote."[2] As we shall see below, there are immensely important differences between voting and custom.

Suárez himself and most of his commentators agree that his thought is best understood in relation to that of Thomas Aquinas and, largely through Aquinas, to the thought of Aristotle.[3] Suárez and his Jesuit commentators emphasize his continuity with many basic doctrines of Aquinas while Suárez's Dominican commentators and many lay Catholic legal theorists and historians emphasize Suárez's innovative breaks with Aquinas.[4] These disputes about whether or not Suárez was a good Thomist would be more illuminating if both sides were to acknowledge that Aquinas's own thought embodied ambiguities and tensions that anticipated and contributed to subsequent scholastic controversies.[5] Because Suárez sought to mediate so many disputes between realists and nominalists, rationalists and voluntarists, it is not surprising that his own nuanced positions are interpreted in opposed ways. Suárez tends to pile on reasons for his positions, and those reasons include Thomistic and non-Thomistic reasons. There is ample evidence in his texts to prove that Suárez both follows carefully and departs radically from the thought of Aquinas.

Usually, Suárez's relation to the legal philosophy of Aquinas is defined in terms of voluntarism and rationalism; but since each thinker defined law in terms of an act involving both reason and will, it is easy to show that there are elements of voluntarism in Aquinas and elements of rationalism in Suárez. I propose a new approach to analyzing the similarities and differences in these two philosophies of law. I will contrast a "semantic" approach to law in Aristotle and Aquinas with a "pragmatic" approach

---

2. Julian: "nam quid interest suffragio populus voluntatem suam declaret an rebus ipsis et factis?" (Digest 1.3.32). Marmor, *Positive Law and Objective Values* 110.

3. One scholar tabulated all of Suárez's citations in the *Metaphysical Disputations*, showing the overwhelming reliance on Aristotle and Aquinas; see Suárez, Ed. John P. Doyle. *On Beings of Reason* (Milwaukee: Marquette University Press, 1995) 11, n. 65.

4. Michel Villey's interpretation has influenced a couple generations of French commentators. Of Suárez's mix of Thomas, Scotus, and Ockham, Villey says "un mélange òu quant au fond, le nominalisme prédomine"; see Michel Villey, *La Formation de la pensée juridique moderne* (Paris: 1975) 376.

5. I show the deep tensions and ambiguities in Aquinas's account of law in Chapter 2 of my *The Philosophy of Positive Law*.

to law in Suárez. Just as there are pragmatic elements to any semantic theory of language and semantic elements in any pragmatic theory, so Aquinas's and Suárez's accounts of law have both semantic and pragmatic elements: my contrast, therefore, is a matter of emphasis. Aquinas sees law as expressing the objective rational and moral order of human life while Suárez sees law as expressing the subjective orders of the legislator. In short, Aquinas asks what a law means while Suárez asks what was meant by it.

Moreover, I will argue that just as semantics is logically prior to pragmatics, so natural law is logically prior to a voluntarist account of law. Semantics is the science of the representation of meaning, and pragmatics is the science of the communication of meaning. Semantics is logically prior to pragmatics because although every act of communication rests upon representation, many kinds of representation involve no act of communication. Within the semantics of the modern theory of the circulation of blood, a pulse represents the heartbeat; but no one thinks that the heart uses the pulse to communicate. A pulse means that the heart is beating but no one asks what the heart meant by a pulse. I will try to show that, at least in the thought of Suárez, the will of the lawmaker cannot be interpreted without recourse to the semantics of the natural law. To answer the question of what a lawmaker subjectively means by his law, Suárez will have to answer the question of what his law objectively means. Customs certainly represent various ideas, values, and purposes, but customs do not necessarily express a will to communicate, let alone endorse, those ideas and values. Customs have a semantics but not a pragmatics: customs no doubt have meaning but nothing determinate is meant by them. Only an author can form an intention to communicate and customs usually have no author.

Semantics and Pragmatics of Law

Aristotle, as we saw, describes the habitual element of custom (*ethos*) as a second nature, and he describes the conventional element of custom (*nomos*) as unwritten law. Not all habits are conventions and not all conventions are habitual, but all customs are habitual conventions and conventional habits. The habitual dimension of custom links it to human nature while the conventional dimension links it to deliberate stipulations, including enacted law. Custom naturalizes social and legal conventions just as it conventionalizes human nature. Custom, thus, must be analyzed in relation to both nature and deliberate stipulation. Thomas Aquinas attempts to capture Aristotle's distinction when he notes that the Latin *mos* can sometimes mean a customary convention (*consuetudo*) and sometimes a quasi-natural habit (*mos* proper).[6] Aquinas also calls customary conventions "unwritten law" and customary habits "second nature," reflecting the way in which custom bridges between nature and law.[7]

Suárez seems to follow Aquinas when he says that *mos* refers to the factual regularities of habit while *consuetudo* refers to the legal element of convention. So *mos* refers to customs of fact, while *consuetudo* refers to customs of law.[8] As so often with Suárez, he is never further away from Aquinas than when he appears to approach him. Aristotle and Aquinas see habit and convention as two aspects or dimensions of every custom: all customs habituate conventions and conventionalize habits. The natural or factual element of habit is inseparable (except in thought) from the cultural or moral element of convention. But Suárez shatters the traditional unity of habit and convention into two mutually exclusive kinds of custom: mere customs of fact and customs of law. One kind of custom is a purely descriptive regularity in human life while the other kind of custom is a prescriptive law. Whereas the natural and factual were intrinsically bonded to the conventional and normative in Aristotle's and Aquinas's theory of custom, for Suárez some customs are merely factual (e.g., all evil customs) while other customs are both factual and lawful, if they are consistent with morality and practiced with an intention that they be obligatory (DL 7, 1.5). In short, Suarez does not merely distinguish two elements within every custom; he distinguishes mere customs of fact from true customs of law.

---

6. "Mos autem duo significat. Quandoque enim significat consuetudinem, sicut dicitur Act. XV, *nisi circumcidamini secundum morem Moysi, non poteritis salvi fieri*. Quandoque vero significat inclinationem quandam naturalem, vel quasi naturalem, ad aliquid agendum, unde etiam et brutorum animalium dicuntur aliqui mores; unde dicitur II Machab. XI, quod *leonum more irruentes in hostes, prostraverunt eos*. Et sic accipitur mos in Psalmo LXVII, ubi dicitur, *qui habitare facit unius moris in domo*." ST I–II, 58.1c.

7. Consuetudo as second nature: ST I–II, 32.2 ad 3; I–II, 58.1c; I–II, 56.5c.

8. "quia mos ad factum tantum refertur, consuetudo vero etiam ad jus" (*De Legibus* Book 7, Chap. 1, sec. 4: hereafter: DL 7, 1.4). Suárez goes on to speak more informally of "consuetudo juris et facti" (DL 7, 1.5). All quotations of Suárez are from the Vivès edition of the *Opera Omnia* (Paris: 1856–1866), 28 vols.; Volumes V and VI contain the *De Legibus*. A critical edition of the *De Legibus* was underway in Madrid, under the direction of Luciano Pereña, but publication ceased in 1981 and it never reached Book VII on custom. James Scott Brown has edited selected parts of the *De Legibus* in his *Selections from Three Works* of Francisco Suárez (New York: Carnegie Endowment for International Peace, 1944). My citation of section numbers follows the Vivès text rather than the slightly different numbered sections in Brown. Where available, I have benefited from the translations in Brown's edition, but I have sought a more consistent rendering of Suárez's technical terms. Many of the sections in Vivès open with the editor's brief synopsis, in Suárez's Latin, of the argument; I sometimes cite these as Suárez when they capture his view succinctly and accurately.

Aquinas follows Aristotle in saying that "law pertains to reason"[9] and that reason is the capacity to discern and to create order: "to be wise is to establish order. The reason for this is that wisdom is the most powerful perfection of reason, whose characteristic is to know order."[10] Aquinas also follows Aristotle in defining law both subjectively, as that which rules and measures; and objectively, as that which is ruled and measured. So law is both the order intrinsic to the world and the rationally apprehended rule by which God and man order the world (ST, I–II, 90.1 ad 1). In his formal account of the kinds of order, Aquinas does not mention Aristotle's triad of natural, customary, and stipulated order. Aquinas says that there are four kinds of order: "the first is the order that reason does not make but only beholds, the order of nature; the second is the order that reason makes in its own acts, as when it arranges concepts and signs of concepts; the third is the order that reason makes in the operation of the will; the fourth is the order that reason makes in the external things it produces." In terms of our Aristotelian triad, Aquinas's four orders actually reduce to two: order independent of human action (the order of nature) and order made by deliberate human action (namely, the order stipulated by reason in thought, deeds, and artifacts). There seems to be nothing corresponding to the order of custom, an order that is the product of human action but not the execution of any design.

In Aristotle and Aquinas, practical reason should order our makings and our actions according to their natural ends; practical reason is artful, but it is art cooperating with nature by subordinating our actions to their intrinsic purposes: "what is proper to moral philosophy is to consider human actions according to how they are ordered to each other and to an end."[11] Human deeds are already intrinsically ordered to their proper ends; practical reason must discern this order and cooperate with it. Aquinas famously says that natural law is the participation of the rational creature in eternal law: through practical reasoning human beings become more or less attuned to the objective order and should seek to cooperate with that order. It is for this reason that Aquinas emphasizes the directive more than the coercive force of law: "Law is a certain rule and measure of acts, according to which a person is led to do something or to refrain" (ST I–II, 90.1c). Law teaches before it commands; the coercive force of law is only

9. "lex est aliquid rationis" ST, I–II, 90.1c.

10. See the prologue to Aquinas's commentary on the Nicomachean Ethics of Aristotle in Corpus Thomisicum, ed. Roberto Busa: http://www.corpusthomisticum.org/

11. See the prologue to Aquinas's commentary on the Nicomachean Ethics of Aristotle in Corpus Thomisicum, ed. Roberto Busa: http://www.corpusthomisticum.org/

necessary because of the recalcitrance due to human sin. Law is essentially directive and educative; it becomes coercive only as a remedy for human sin. In this teaching and directive capacity, civil laws are like the laws of grammar or of various arts: they induce us to act well by attuning us to the objective structure of human making and conduct.

If law for Aquinas means creatively adapting our conduct to the objective moral order, then law for Suárez means giving orders. Instead of expressing the intrinsic or natural order, law for Suárez expresses the will of the lawgiver.[12] This is the contrast between law as a rule and measure of what is already intrinsically ordered and law as a precept giving normative force to a course of conduct. The difference between Aquinas and Suárez is subtler than the crude contrasts between reason and will, or between the objective and the subjective, or between directive and coercive force of law.[13] After all, Aquinas also describes law as a precept stemming from the will and reason of the lawgiver, and Suárez also claims that law prohibits many actions because they are intrinsically evil. Both acknowledge the directive and the coercive force of law. Nonetheless, I think it fair to say there are significant contrasts in their accounts of law. How to characterize these differences? I think it helpful to borrow an ancient distinction in the philosophy of language between semantic and pragmatic approaches to meaning. In ancient logic and modern semantics, the focus is on what words and propositions mean, that is, what objects they represent. Here linguistic signs are assimilated to the wider universe of signs, such as symptoms and other natural signs: we ask what a pulse means just as we might ask what a sentence means. Logic and semantics study how linguistic and other signs represent objects. But language is not only a system of representational signs; it is also a mode of communication. In ancient rhetoric and modern pragmatics the unit of analysis is not a word or proposition but a speech act, an assertion, permission, command, and so forth. Here we ask not what a word or proposition means but rather what was meant by it. Language is assimilated to other modes of communication, such as gestures or animal grunts. Just as we might ask of a slammed door, "what did he mean by that?" so we might ask the same

12. The *jeu de mots* in the contrast between law expressing objective order and law giving orders is found in Courtine, Jean-François. *Nature et empire de la loi* (Paris: J. Vrin, 1999) 95.

13. For example, Michel Bastit strongly emphasizes the contrast between Aquinas's "regula et mensura" and Suárez's "preceptum"; Bastit even observes that the term "precept" is absent in Aquinas's definition of law. But Aquinas does frequently refer to laws as precepts (e.g. ST I–II, 90.2 ad 1), so this contrast is overdrawn. Michel Bastit, *Naissance de la loi moderne* (Paris: Presses Universitaires de France, 1990) 314.

of a sentence. But we would not ask of a symptom or of a darkening sky, "what was meant by that?" Semantic and pragmatic meanings can diverge radically so that what a sentence means can be quite opposed to what was meant by it, as in sarcasm. In the interpretation of statutes, some lawyers focus on the semantic question of what the statute itself means while other lawyers focus on the pragmatic question of what the legislator meant by it. Some theories of semantics attempt to incorporate the pragmatic dimension of language by bringing the speaker's meaning into the analysis of representation; and some theories of pragmatics attempt to incorporate the representational dimension of language into their analysis of communication. But philosophers disagree about the extent to which semantic and pragmatic approaches to language can be reconciled;[14] and jurists continue to disagree about whether judges should look to what a statute means or to what the legislator meant by it.

Aquinas's legal theory essentially focuses on the basic logical question of what a law means rather than what a legislator meant by it. Aquinas's whole analogical treatment of the meaning of law, ranging from the eternal law through both natural and divine law into human civil and canon law understands law primarily as a rational representation of an objective divine and natural order. Aquinas also distinguishes the rational from the real basis of law when he says that law is present not only in the reason of the lawgiver but also in the intrinsic finality of what is subject to law (ST, I–II, 90.1 ad 1and 91.2c): "law is a rule and measure . . . and has a two-fold existence: in the thing ruling and measuring and in the thing ruled and measured." Elsewhere Aquinas distinguishes *ius* as the objective order of what is just from *lex* as the subjective rational grasp of that order in thought: *lex non est ipsum ius, proprie loquendo, sed aliqualis ratio juris* (ST, II–II, 57.1 ad 2). For example, in the world of business, what is intrinsically just and lawful (*ius*) is an exchange of things of equivalent value; the subjective formulation of this equality in a precept of the just price is law (*lex*). The authoritative precept regulates conduct by expressing what is inherently just. This view of law as expressive of objective order brings civil law

---

14. F. Strawson has described the conflict between semantics and pragmatics as "a Homeric struggle," but John Searle thinks it a "mistake" to "suppose that the two theories are necessarily in conflict." Yet Searle is squarely in the pragmatic camp when he says that the basic unit of language is not a word or sentence but a speech act. See Searle, *Speech Acts* (Cambridge: Cambridge University Press, 1969) 16 and "Meaning, Communication, and Representation" in *Philosophical Grounds of Rationality*, Eds. Richard E. Grandy and Richard Warner (Oxford: Clarendon Press, 1986) 209–226 at 225. For an analysis of semantics and pragmatics in scholastic logic, see James B. Murphy, "Language, Communication and Representation in the Semiotic of John Poinsot" *The Thomist* 58/4 (October 1994) 569–598.

into relation with other kinds of rules, such as the "laws" of grammar or the "laws" of carpentry: the rules of grammar or carpentry do not express the will of a grammarian or a carpenter; they express the objective order of operations in those arts. The successful grammarian or carpenter must attune his conduct to the objective requirements of those arts, just as a successful legislator must attune his conduct to the objective requirements of the common good.[15] Just as natural law is rooted in the objective moral order and customary law is rooted in the objective order of custom, so enacted law is rooted in the objective order of stipulation. Aquinas agrees that enacted law expresses not only the objective requirements of the common good, but also the intentional choice of the legislator doesn't define all law in terms of this legislative intention. Instead of seeing stipulated order as resting on natural and customary order, Suárez attempts to define natural and customary law as kinds of stipulated law, manifesting the will of the legislator.

Suárez interprets law, not in terms of the semantics of different kinds of order, but in terms of the pragmatics of moral action. Law for him is the act of giving orders; order always signifies the activity of a divine or human lawgiver.[16] He rejects the analogy between law and the technical arts; for him law is a specifically moral kind of practical reason. Law is not like the ordered operations of an art, but like the precepts, counsels, and commands whereby superiors guide the moral conduct of inferiors. He frequently says that the essence of law is the will or intention of the legislator.[17] Nowhere does he put this more forcefully than when he says, "the will of the legislator is the intrinsic form and soul of law. This is because law essentially depends for its existence and institution on the intention of the legislator."[18] In short, law gets its meaning, not from the objective order of human life, but from the will of the legislator: law does not express order, it gives orders. Here Suárez cites with approval Ulpian's famous tag that "whatever pleases the prince has the force of law"—a view Aquinas accepts only with deep qualification.[19] Suárez bases his claim about the

---

15. According to Aquinas, "l'agir suit l'être": I. André-Vincent, "La notion moderne de droit naturel et le voluntarisme," *Archives de philosophie de droit* 8 (1963) 237–259 at 241.

16. "ordinatio autem activa est a legislatore, et ille actus quo ordinat, appellatur ordinatio activa. . . ." (DL 1, 12.3).

17. "Verba sunt materia et corpus legis; mens legislatoris anima" (DL 3, 20.1).

18. "Voluntas legislatoris est intrinseca forma et anima legis. Probatur, quia lex essentialiter pendet in suo esse ac institutione ab intentione legislatoris" (DL 3, 20.3).

19. "Quod principi placuit, legis habet vigorem": see the *Digest of Justinian*, Latin text ed. Theodor Mommsen and Paul Krueger, English translation edited by Alan Watson (Philadelphia: University of Pennsylvania Press, 1985) I, 4.1. Note that Ulpian claims here only that the will of the prince has the force of law, not that it is law (lex); he calls the commands of the Emperors "constitutiones." For Aquinas's reservations about Ulpian's claim see ST, I–II, 90.1 ad 3.

will of the legislator on his understanding of the nature of all moral actions, including that of giving law: "every moral act depends essentially on the intention [of the agent], without which there is no true moral act."[20] So from a Thomistic premise, that every moral act gets its species from the intention of the agent, Suárez draws a distinctly non-Thomistic conclusion, namely, that will is the essence of law. As the argument stands in the *De Legibus*, it is a non sequitur; what are missing are the arguments to show that intentions belong solely to the faculty of the will and not also of reason. As is well known, in order to save the freedom of the will from the determinism of the intellect, Suárez tended to reduce reason to an extrinsic role in moral operations. According to Suárez, says Thomas Mullaney, "reason does not enter in as a *per se* cause of a free act."[21] So Suárez can move from the widely accepted view that moral acts depend essentially upon the intention of the agent to his legal voluntarism only by means of his own very controversial arguments about the relation of reason to will in moral acts. Suárez's legal voluntarism also seems to rest upon his linguistic voluntarism: he says that "all the words of human laws signify according to the will and from the imposition of the legislator."[22] If the very words used by a legislator get their meaning from the will, then, a fortiori, law must stem from the will as well.

Suárez claims that by grounding law in his general theory of moral action, he achieves a more precise and univocal definition of law than Aquinas offers. Suárez opens his treatise on laws with a revealing misquotation of Aquinas: "Law is a certain rule and measure according to which someone is led to do something or refrain from doing something."[23] This definition of law is quite broad and Suárez takes Aquinas to task for offering a definition that not only includes rules of the arts, counsel, and many other kinds of practical reason, but that also applies to both rational and nonrational creatures. Yet Suárez has omitted a key word in Aquinas's actual definition of law: "acts [of men]." In short, although Aquinas uses the term "law" in wider analogical senses, he defines the central case of

20. "Ratio est, quia omnis actus moralis pendet essentialiter ab intentione, sine qua non est verus actus" (DL, 3, 20.3).

21. "Suárez explicitly says that freedom is in the will alone formally... knowledge, he says, concurs as a merely accidental cause to my appetite..." Thomas Mullaney, *Suárez on Human Freedom* (Baltimore: The Carroll Press, 1950) x and xi.

22. "enim omnia verba humanorum legum ad placitum et ex impositione significare" DL 6, 1.9. For Suárez's view that "significatio vocum et nominum, non est naturalis, sed ad placitum," see *Tractatus De Divina Substantia* 2, 31.4 in Vivès Vol. 1.

23. The translator of the Brown edition of Suárez notes the discrepancy but says only: "This quotation, as given by Suárez, varies from St. Thomas's text." See Brown, *Selections from Three Works* 21.

law in relation to the deliberate moral acts of man.[24] If Suárez had correctly quoted Aquinas, then his opening critique would lose all of its force since Aquinas does define law centrally in relation to human moral actions. On this point, Suárez and Aquinas are in heated agreement.

If positive law were the exemplar of all law, then one can see why Suárez defines law in terms of the will rather than of reason. According to Suárez, natural law concerns what is prohibited because it is evil, while positive law concerns what is evil because prohibited.[25] It is for this reason that Suárez will claim that the law of nations is positive and not natural law (DL 2, 19). He argues that the subject matter of positive law is conduct that is morally indifferent: reason can detect no moral distinction between doing or refraining from activities that are morally indifferent. Since the distinctions made by positive law, then, do not rest upon intrinsic and rational moral differences, they must rest simply on the will and fiat of the legislator. Suárez cites as an example of a morally indifferent action the decision of a man whether to carry weapons in a certain place or not (DL 1, 9.5). Here we see the deep problems associated with the whole notion of "things indifferent": although in the abstract, it may be morally indifferent whether I carry a weapon, in the context of actual human choices, it is never morally different.[26] The concrete choice for a legislator is to decide whether, given these men, these customs, these circumstances, the common good is best secured by permitting or forbidding the carrying of weapons. Suárez imagines reason paralyzed, like Buridan's Ass, when faced with intrinsically indifferent alternatives, until the will makes its free and rationally underdetermined fiat.[27] Similarly, to protect the freedom of

---

24. Here is Suarez's quotation of Aquinas at ST I–II, 90.1c: "Lex est quaedam regula et mensura, secundam quam inducitur aliquis ad agendum, vel ab agendo retrahitur." DL 1, 1.1. The Vivès text corresponds perfectly to the text of the 1612 Coimbra edition. Here is Aquinas's actual definition of law: "Respondeo dicendum quod lex quaedam regula est et mensura actuum, secundum quam inducitur aliquis ad agendum, vel ab agendo retrahitur, dicitur enim lex a ligando, quia obligat ad agendum. Regula autem et mensura humanorum actuum est ratio, quae est primum principium actuum humanorum, ut ex praedictis patet, rationis enim est ordinare ad finem, qui est primum principium in agendis, secundum philosophum." Neither the Leonine edition nor Busa's edition of Aquinas indicates any textual variants for this passage. For Aquinas's analysis of the acts of men, see ST, I–II, 6.1 ff.

25. "intrinsece malum": (DL 1, 9.3); "malum quia prohibitum": (DL 1, 9.4). For a philosophical critique of this distinction in relation to Thomas Aquinas, see James B. Murphy, *Philosophy of Positive Law* 106–110.

26. For a philosophical critique of the notion of "things indifferent" in relation to Aquinas, see Murphy, *Philosophy of Positive Law* 102–106.

27. For Suarez's discussion of the "freedom of indifferents" see his *Disputationes Metaphysicae*, Dis 19, II, 11–15: "Signum ergo est hunc varium operandi modum formaliter seu proxime non consistere in discursu et apprehensione rationis, sed in libertate vel indifferentia" (par. 15).

the will from the determinism of reason, Suárez is much more concerned than is Aquinas to distinguish law from mere counsel. The rational content of a counsel and a law might be identical; they can be distinguished only by reference to the will of the preceptor.[28] When I give counsel, I do not demand conformity as when I lay down a precept of law. Of course, not everyone can give law, only our superiors have this authority; but law cannot be defined as whatever rules are made by our superiors, because superiors often offer counsel as well as law. A superior must intend that his rules be understood as obligatory and enforced as such: "law gets from the will of the prince its efficacy and obligatory force" (DL 6, 9.4).[29] To protect the intrinsic freedom of the moral act, Suárez makes law into a purely extrinsic constraint.[30]

Sometimes Suárez defines law as an act of the will of the legislator and sometimes as a sign manifesting that act of will.[31] In some places, he distinguishes the "body" of the law (*corpus legis*) as the external verbal signs from the soul of the law (*anima legis*) as the will of the prince (DL 3, 15.1; DL 3, 20.1). The civil law, he says, belongs to the genus of sign of the will of the prince.[32] The body of the law belongs to the genus of sign while the soul of the law belongs to the genus of act of will. Indeed, Suárez offers two formal definitions of law, one corresponding to the will's act itself and the other to a sign of that will. In one place Suárez defines law as "the act of a just and upright will, whereby a superior obliges an inferior to do this or that"; in another place he defines law as a verbal sign of that will, "a general precept, just and durable, sufficiently promulgated."[33] Sometimes, however, the plain meaning of the verbal signs is inconsistent with the intention of the legislator: in these cases, an interpreter of law must choose between what the law means and what was meant by it.

---

28. For Suárez's view that "concilium non esse veram legem" see DL 1, 1.1; 1, 1.8 and 1, 14.

29. "habet enim voluntas superioris hanc moralem efficacitatem, ut possit obligare subditos…" DL 1, 4.9.

30. "On saisit très clairement ici le paradox auquel aboutit Suárez: puisque l'acte doit être libre, la loi doit être obligatoire et donc non immanente, mais imposées de l'extérieur par une force coercitive." Bastit, *Naissance de la loi modern* 313.

31. Suárez cites Gabriel with approval: "definit legem esse signum principis voluntatem vel mentem sufficienter manifestans." DL 1, 4.4. Later, Suárez says: "Nam, sicut lex constituitur in ratione legis humanae, quatenus est signum voluntatis praeceptivae seu obligantis…" DL 3, 20.8.

32. "legem civilem quae subditis datur constitui in genere signi indicantis principis voluntatem" (DL 3, 15.1).

33. Suárez's two formal definitions of law: "legem mentalem (ut sic dicam) in ipso legislatore esse actum voluntatis justae et rectae, quo superior vult inferiorem obligare ad hoc vel illud faciendum" DL 1, 5, 24; "Lex est commune praeceptum, justum ac stabile, sufficienter promulgatum" DL 1, 12.4.

But in one very intriguing passage, Suárez says that the words manifesting a law cannot be the essence of law, since they refer to the will of the prince, which is more essentially law. So far, this is just the common claim of legal voluntarism. Then Suárez pushes the inquiry in a deeper, semantic direction. He says that the will of the prince is itself a sign, so the true essence of law must be found in what is signified by the will of the prince.[34] Here Suárez implicitly distinguishes between instrumental and formal signs: the spoken or written words of a law are instrumental signs of the will of the prince (formulated in mental words or concepts) while the will of the prince itself refers to objects, both real and rational. For example, if the prince aims to support or to suppress a custom, then his will refers both to that actual custom and to some reason for either supporting or suppressing it. According to Suárez here, the essence of law would be found in the actual practices and norms that are signified by the will of the prince. In one place, he summarizes these three approaches to the essence of law by distinguishing three places in which law may be found: in the mind of the legislator, in the conduct of his subject, or in some visible sign manifesting the will of a superior (DL 1, 4.4).

Suárez distinguishes three kinds of legal interpretation: authentic, usual [i.e., customary], and doctrinal (DL 6, 1.1).[35] An interpretation is authentic if it comes from the legislator himself; usual, if it comes from custom; and doctrinal, if it comes from the teaching of learned jurists. What unifies these different modes of interpretation is that they all aim to discern the will of the legislator. Authentic interpretation by the original lawgiver has its authority from the will of the legislator: since a legislator can abrogate a law at will, then a fortiori, he can interpret it. Similarly, since custom, which expresses the legislative will of the people, has the authority to establish new law, a fortiori, it can interpret law.[36] Suárez says that judicial

---

34. "Nec etiam dici potest locutionem illam internam, prout consideratur in mente principis, esse legem, quia etiam illa solum habet vim et efficaciam, quatenus est signum: ergo necessario supponit id quod principaliter est lex" (DL 1, 5.6). The distinction between formal and instrumental signs was developed by late medieval scholastic commentators on Aristotle's *Perihermenias*: instrumental signs (such as spoken or written words) must be cognized as objects before they can refer to something; formal signs (such as concepts) refer the mind to their objects without having first been cognized as objects. Suárez may well have learned his semiotics from the Jesuits of Coimbra. See John Doyle, *The Conimbricenses: some questions on Signs* (Milwaukee: Marquette University Press, 2001).

35. My discussion of Suárez's view of the interpretation of law owes much to John Doyle's paper "Francisco Suárez on the Interpretation of Laws," in *The Modern Schoolman* 83/3 (March 2006) 197–222. Also in John P. Doyle, *Collected Studies on Francisco Suárez, S. J. (1548–1617)*, Ed. Victor M. Salas (Leuven, Belgium: Leuven University Press, 2010) 357–387.

36. "quia non est necessaria major auctoritas, nec expressior voluntas ad interpretandam legem jam factum, quam ad novam introducendam…" (DL 7, 17.1).

interpretation of a law is one kind of customary interpretation and that among the various kinds of customary interpretations, judicial interpretations are the best evidence of the will of the people.[37] Custom may also interpret divine law by indicating the will of the divine law giver, as manifested by universal Church practice.[38] Finally, custom may interpret itself, since it is the best evidence of the legislative will of the people (DL 7, 17.6). Doctrinal interpretation is necessary, says Suárez, because ambiguity and vagueness are pervasive in human language, meaning that doubts will often arise about the proper application of a law to new circumstances (DL 6, 1.6).

The relation of the words of a law to the will of the legislator is complex and requires the expert judgment of jurists.[39] Although the will of the legislator is the soul of law (DL 6, 1.12), we have access to that will mainly through the words of the law. Only jurists, for example, can distinguish between the ordinary and the technical meaning of words in a law. Suárez distinguishes the natural from the civil meaning of words. By "natural," he refers to the ordinary customary meaning, which he describes as stemming from the stipulation of the community.[40] By "civil" he refers to the technical legal meaning. Normally, the words of a law reliably manifest the will of the legislator, so we must presume that a lawgiver uses words in their ordinary customary sense.[41] Words are prior to will in the order of knowing, so we should rely upon the words of a statue to manifest the will; but will is prior to words in the order of being, so that ultimately we must prefer knowledge of the will to that of the words. Because the will of the legislator is harder to know than his words, normally we should prefer the words ("ergo praeferenda sunt verba per se loquendo, vel saltem regulariter," DL 6, 1.15). But where the words of a law seem to contradict the presumed or known will of a legislator, then we must prefer the will to the words: "ergo voluntas verbis praeferenda" (DL 6, 1.16).

Whether law is defined in terms of the will or the reason of the lawgiver, there are some shortcomings to any account of law rooted in deliberate

37. "nam sententiae ipsae ad hoc maxime valent, quatenus communi consensu populi recipiuntur et probantur..." (DL 7, 17.4).

38. "Divinam autem solum interpretatur, indicando legislatoris mentem, et ideo, ut certa sit oportet ut consuetudo sit universalis Ecclesiae traditio..." (DL 7, 17.6).

39. "ex hac necessitate orta est juris civilis peritia, cujus praecipuus finis est verum sensum veramque interpretationem legum humanarum tradere" (DL 6, 1.5).

40. "omnia verba humanarum legum ad placitum et ex impositione significare..." (DL 6, 1.9). How Aristotle's argument—that words get their meaning from "customary convention" (kata sunthēkēn)—was translated into Latin as "deliberate stipulation" (ad placitum et ex impositione), is a long story: for some details, see Murphy, *Philosophy of Positive Law* 44–47.

41. "quia legislator censetur uti verbis juxta communem usum..." (DL 7, 17.5).

stipulation by a legislator. Some kinds of law, such as the law that arises from precedents or from custom, are not the product of anyone's deliberate stipulation. In the Aristotelian tradition, the kinds of law reflect the diversity of irreducible kinds of order: natural order, customary order, and stipulated order. To define law in terms of stipulated order is to attempt to reduce the natural and customary order to the order of deliberate stipulation. Aristotle himself often reduces customary order to natural order ("second nature") and to the order of deliberate stipulation ("unwritten law"). We shall find Suárez attempting to reduce the order of custom to the order of deliberate stipulation. Indeed, both Aquinas and Suárez will find it very difficult to describe the diversity of the kinds of law, since they both have adopted the word "*lex*" as their primary word for law. In the language of the Roman jurists, a *lex* is but one kind of law (*ius*), namely, a statute. Roman lawyers distinguished several fundamentally different kinds of law: natural, customary, and stipulated; the role of a jurist is to harmonize these heterogeneous kinds of norm into a coherent body of *ius*. Even today our lawyers will say that the law (*ius*) of contracts includes statutes (*leges*), natural moral principles, precedents, and legal doctrines. A lawyer would not flatten the heterogeneity of his sources by saying that the law of contracts is a collection of laws. But Aquinas and Suárez both stipulate that by law they mean *lex*, so that all kinds of law become statutory in form: *lex naturalis* and *lex consuetudinis*.[42] Both Aquinas and Suárez explicitly define ius as a moral not a legal term: for Aquinas it is what is objectively just and for Suárez it is a subjective moral power.[43] As we shall see, Suárez will attempt to develop a statutory theory of law, including natural law and customary law. We will also see that there is something odd about a statute of nature or a statute of custom.

If all law is a statute, then both the diversity and the hierarchy of laws will reflect the diversity and hierarchy of lawgivers. In Aquinas, the diversity of laws reflects the diversity of the kinds of order: natural law signifies the order of nature, especially the structure of inclinations in human rational nature; customary law reflects the tacit order of habitual human conventions; positive law reflects the order deliberately stipulated by the prince. Aquinas's inquiry into the kinds of law is guided by the question: what objective order does law and ought law to signify? In Suárez, by contrast,

---

42. For a philosophical exploration of the contrast between the lawyer's *ius* and the philosopher's *lex*, see James B. Murphy, "The Lawyer and the Layman: Two Perspectives on the Rule of Law" *Review of Politics* 68 (Winter 2006) 101–131.

43. For Aquinas on ius as "quod est iustum" see ST, II–II, 57.1c; for Suárez on ius as a "facultas moralis" see DL 1, 2.5.

the diversity of laws reflects the diversity of lawgivers. Natural and divine law signify the will of God while civil and canon law signify the will of men. As we shall see, on his account, customary law differs from positive law, not because the order of custom differs from deliberately stipulated order, but because customary law has a different lawgiver from positive law.

It makes sense to think of divine law and of positive law (civil or canon) as reflecting the will of the lawgiver, since these kinds of law are deliberately made and imposed. But natural law and customary law are not made or imposed but grow up spontaneously and reflect the intrinsic properties of human nature and conventions. To the extent that human nature and conventions change over time, so do natural and customary law. But Suárez interprets natural and customary law as if it were made and imposed by a lawgiver. In short, for Suárez, all law is legislation: "without will, there is no law."[44] He says, "the natural law as it exists in us is a sign of some particular will of God."[45] Suárez anticipates Hobbes when he argues that a law must promulgate, not only the content of a precept, but also the authority of the lawgiver. If legal obligation rests upon a chain of command, then subjects must be told not just what to do but also by whose authority they are to do it. Suárez argues that natural law signifies not only the will of God, but also the identity of God as our sovereign lawgiver. In discerning the natural law, we learn not only what is commanded but also who commanded it.[46] Sometimes Suárez sounds like Aquinas when he distinguishes natural law from positive law on the grounds that natural law prohibits what is intrinsically evil while positive law prohibits what is evil because prohibited. How do we distinguish these two kinds of evil? In a few places, Suárez says that intrinsic evil is not consonant with our nature and that we should avoid what is not consonant with our nature (DL 2, 7.1 and 9.4). But more often Suárez says that we should avoid intrinsic evil because it is not consonant with God's will: intrinsic evil must violate God's will since God cannot be irrational or unjust.[47] Indeed, given Suárez's view of obligation, the mere fact that something is consonant with our nature would

---

44. "ergo lex naturalis Dei voluntatem includit, quia sine voluntate non est legislatio." DL 2, 6.10.

45. "ergo lex naturalis in nobis existens est signum alicujus voluntatis Dei." DL 2, 6.10. Suárez cites Gerson with approval: "lex naturalis praeceptiva est signum inditum cuilibet homini non impedito in usu debito rationis, et notificativum voluntatis divinae volentis. . . ." DL 2, 6.5.

46. "ergo lex naturalis, prout in homine est, non solum indicat rem ipsam in se, sed etiam ut prohibitam, vel praeceptam ab aliquo superiori. . . " DL 2, 6.7. "ergo ratio naturalis, quae indicat quid sit per se malum vel bonum homini, consequenter indicat esse secundum divinam voluntatem ut unum fiat, et aliud vitetur." DL 2, 6.8.

47. "quia voluntas Dei non potest esse irrationalibilis. . . " DL 2, 6.8. "quia cum haec [lex naturalis] sit vera lex, et Deum habeat auctorem, non potest non esse honestum. . . " DL, 2, 7.1.

furnish no duty to do it. As Suárez frequently observes, the existence of a precept is quite distinct from the question of its obligatory force.[48] Although for Aquinas a natural law precept gets its obligatory force from its intrinsic relation to the common good, for Suárez all obligation stems from the will of a superior.[49] Despite the evident voluntarism of his theory of obligation, Suárez rejects the radical voluntarism of Ockham and affirms a more nuanced position (DL 2, 6.4, 6.20, 15.3, 15.4).

Suárez's classifications of law are complex, subtle, overlapping, and confusing. The reason is that he has inherited several traditional sets of classification that he discusses but then quietly drops. Yet he does not set forth his own distinctive logic of classification, based on the diversity of lawgivers, very explicitly. He begins with the distinction between eternal law and temporal law (DL 1, 3.6), but fails to elaborate. Since eternal law for him exists only in God's mind and outside Creation, it has no bearing on the providential government of any creature; insofar as all law governs creatures, all law is temporal.[50] He also discusses the traditional distinction between natural and positive law on the traditional grounds that natural law is intrinsic and positive law extrinsic to human nature (DL 1, 3.15). But this distinction is not and cannot be central to his legal thought because for him natural law is just another mode of divine law, as we have seen; and positive law is imposed by both the divine and human legislators.[51] Given Suárez's legal voluntarism, the only possible basis for the diversity of law must be the diversity of lawgivers. And so when Suárez distinguishes divine from human positive law, he rightly observes that there can be no other kinds of positive law relating to man because there are no other legislators.[52] Of human positive law, Suárez says that it is human not because it governs the temporal, or secular order, but because it is imposed by human

48. "quia aliud est loqui de existentia praeceptorum (ut sic dicam) aliud de actuali obligatione, seu exercitio eorum." DL 2, 8.8.

49. "Nam si in lege attendatur vis movendi, et ideo lex dicatur id quod est in principe, quod movet et obligat ad agendum, sic lex est actus voluntatis. . . ." DL 1, 5.21.

50. Eternal law cannot be true law because "if it is eternal, it can only be located in the mind of God and is therefore no true 'law.' If it is a law, it must be established, promulgated and imposed on subjects, in which case it cannot be 'eternal'." Pauline C. Westerman, *The Disintegration of Natural Law Theory* (Leiden: Brill, 1998) 84–85.

51. Aquinas, in the ST, resisted referring to Mosaic law as divine positive law, even though he did so earlier in his commentary on the propositions of Peter Lombard. More important, Aquinas's account of positive law applies perfectly to much of Mosaic law, and his account of the ceremonial Mosaic law perfectly parallels his account of human positive law. On divine and human positive law in Aquinas, see Murphy, *Philosophy of Positive Law* 50–54. Suárez, by contrast, devotes the 9th Book of his treatise on laws to the "old [Mosaic] divine positive law."

52. "Praeter has vero non potest esse alia positive lex respectu hominum, quia non sunt plures legislatores" DL 1, 3.15.

legislators.[53] Suárez then divides human positive law into civil and canon law, reflecting the difference between princely and papal legislators (DL 1, 3.21). The clearest statement of Suárez's innovative classification of laws comes in his discussion of how to classify the law of nations. Yet even this statement manifests the confusion of Suárez moving from traditional to new kinds of distinctions: "law is adequately divided into natural and positive, properly speaking, or (*vel*) into divine and human, both sides of the divides named by their author and both sides being mutually exclusive."[54] By conjoining these two sets of distinctions with *vel*, Suárez implies that they are equivalent; yet by his own account elsewhere, positive law cuts across the distinction between divine and human law. Moreover, natural law and positive law are not divided by their authors as are divine and human law; nor are natural law and positive law mutually exclusive, even though Aquinas and Suárez often describe them so.[55] True, even Homer nods, but I think these muddles reveal Suárez's attempt to shift from a traditional to a voluntarist logic of classification.

For Aquinas, natural and divine law are prior in logical generality to the specifications of civil and canon law, but for Suárez, natural and divine law are prior to civil and canon law because God is superior to man. The hierarchy of laws in Aquinas is based on the objective and inherent priority of general principle to particular rule; just as the civil law makes concrete the law of nature, so the canon law makes concrete the law of love. But Suárez describes the hierarchy of laws as a chain of command: civil and canon law are subordinate to natural and divine law because man is subordinate to God.[56] Lower-level laws are valid only if authorized by higher-level lawgivers: since God commands that we obey just human law, our duty to obey even human law stems from our duty to obey God.[57] Indeed, for Suárez the very notion of an obligation involves by conceptual necessity a relation between a superior and an inferior.[58] And Suárez's

---

53. "Superest dicendum de lege positive humana. . . . dicitur ergo humana lex, quia proxime ab hominibus inventa et posita est" DL 1, 3.18.

54. "quia lex sufficienter dividitur per naturalem et positivam proprie dictam, vel per divinam et humanam ab auctore utramque denominando, quia utraque membra immediatam contradictionem involvunt, ut constat. . ." DL 2, 19. 4.

55. For Aquinas's treatment of natural and positive law as mutually exclusive, despite the logic of his own theory, see Murphy, *Philosophy of Positive Law* 89–113.

56. André-Vincent makes this point in his "La notion moderne de droit naturel et le volontarisme," 243.

57. "Nam quia vis obligandi legis humanae principaliter nititur in lege aeterna, ideo qui illam transgreditur, virtute violat legem aeternam et divinam, et hoc modo convenit etiam illi transgressioni definitio peccati" (DL 3, 21.15).

58. "habet enim voluntas superioris hanc moralem efficacitatem, ut possit obligare subditos. . ." (DL 1, 4.9.

notion of legal obligation includes by conceptual necessity the power of a superior to coerce his inferiors: the essential effect of law is its coercive power.[59] So neither the prince nor the pope can abrogate a precept of natural law, because all human legislators are subject to divine power.[60] Suárez frequently explains the nature of legal obligation in terms of a hierarchy of power.[61]

Custom: Will of the Sovereign?

Suárez's vast exploration of customary law has one essential aim: to show that the law that arises from custom is not different in any significant way from the law that is imposed by the supreme legislator in any polity. His task is made immeasurably more difficult by the voluntarism of his account of law. Although it is at least prima facie plausible to regard legislation as the will and command of the supreme political authority, Suárez seeks to prove that custom is equally the will and command of the supreme political authority. Since statutes are deliberately made while customs arise, not from design, but as a by-product of human social conduct, it seems odd to describe customs as the command of the legislator. As we shall see, Suárez's attempt to do so both reveals and obscures the nature of custom. Commentary on Suárez's view of the law of nations typically says little about his theory of custom; and commentary on his theory of custom typically says little about this view of the law of nations. Indeed, although Suárez himself claims that the law of nations is customary, he rarely attempts to relate what he says about the law of nations in Books 2 and 3 with his formal account of custom in Book 7.

Suárez frequently insists that customary law is just as much a sign of the will of the legislator as is statutory law. The only difference between a statute and a custom, he says, is the insignificant difference in how that will is signified: a statute is signified by words while a custom is signified by deeds.[62] In all essential respects, there is no difference between a custom

---

59. "quia proprius effectus legis est ligare, seu obligare" (DL 1, 1.9); "cum de ratione legis sit obligare" (DL 2, 4.2).

60. "in omni praecepto juris naturalis legislator est Deus; sed non potest homo mutare legem quam Deus tulit, quia inferior non potest praevalere contra superiorem" (DL 2, 14.8).

61. "Inferior non potest tollere legem superioris" (DL 6, 14.4); "superior legem inferioris abrogare potest" (DL 6, 26.2); "inferior non potest abrogare legem superioris" (DL 6, 26.4)

62. "quia haec lex consuetudinis per se non differ ab illa [lex scripta], nisi in signo sensibili, quo explicatur voluntas legislatoris (quod signum voco sensibilem formam legis)...hic vero non est signum scriptum, nec ita expressum, sed sunt facta externa, ut declaratum est" (DL 7, 16.1).

and a statute: they must both be morally sound, conducive to the common good, and reasonable.[63] Both custom and statute are mainly dependent on the will of the prince who possesses the power of legislation: his power is the efficient cause and his will is the formal cause of both kinds of law.[64] Suárez says that three elements are necessary and sufficient for all law, including custom: appropriate subject matter, power, and a will adequately signified.[65] Indeed, in one respect custom seems to be even more lawful than legislation: for whereas words are mere conventional signs of the will of the prince, customs are natural signs of his will.[66] Suárez does not develop this thought, but one might observe that conventional signs change rapidly over time and make deception easy, while natural signs are durable and less suitable for deception. Augustine and Hobbes famously argue, for example, that the countenance is more truthful than is speech.[67]

Because customs are not designed or made by any one person, what kind of will or intention do they signify? No one wills custom into being as a legislator might will a statute into being. Customs simply arise willy-nilly. If customs are not deliberately made, perhaps they are deliberately chosen? Yet we acquire many of our customs prior to our awareness or knowledge of them, like the custom of speaking our native tongue. Sometimes we deliberately choose our customs, but often they choose us. What does will have to do with custom? Once we are aware of our customs, we can choose to affirm them or reject them. If, once aware of a custom, we then continue to practice it, we could be said to consent to it in the sense of affirming it. Compared to notions like "design" or "make" or "choose," consent is a minimal exercise of will. But Suárez's claim that custom signifies the will of the prince rests upon his understanding of consent. To some extent, Suárez builds the notion of consent into his definition of custom: he defines custom as a free moral action.[68] Because Suárez says that usages that rest upon ignorance, fraud, or coercion are by definition not

---

63. "In caeteris vero causis non est differentia inter has leges [i.e. scripta et non scripta], cum proportione de illis loquendo, quia de materia jam dictum est debere esse honestam, communi bono accommodatum, ac denique rationabilem" (DL 7, 16.1).
64. "utramque etiam maxime pendere a voluntate principis habentis potestatem legislativam, quae est in utraque propria causa efficiens, et voluntate est quasi intrinseca forma" (DL 7, 16.1).
65. "quia ad legem tria vel quatuor sunt necessaria et sufficient, scilicet, materia proportionata, potestas, et voluntas sufficienter exterius significata, et haec omnia possunt in hac consuetudine concurrere" (DL 7, 14.3).
66. "ex communi acceptione et quasi naturali significatione, receptum est hoc signum consuetudinis tanquam sufficiens ad indicandam talem populi voluntatem..." (DL 7, 14.8).
67. Augustine, *De Doctrina Christiana* II, 1, 2 cols. 36–37 in *Patrologia Latina*; Hobbes, *Leviathan* 6.56.
68. "Propria enim consuetudo non est nisi in actibus liberis..." (DL 7, 1.4).

customs, it becomes tautological to claim that customs are voluntary in some sense.[69] But Suárez asserts some very strong claims about the voluntary nature of custom that are far from tautological: about those customs justifiably treated as lawful, he claims that both the people practicing a custom and the supreme legislator consent to the custom; that by consent he means more than toleration or passive acquiescence but active approval of a custom; and that when our approval of a custom includes the intention that the custom be enforced as mandatory, we have arrived at a lawful custom.

Suárez was certainly not the first to argue that customs are justified as lawful because they rest upon consent. That idea stems from the Roman jurists. He cites Julian's famous quip: "What does it matter whether the people express their will by voting or by their deeds themselves?"[70] The Roman jurist Hermogenianus also describes custom as the "silent agreement of the citizens."[71] But these ideas pre-date the classical Roman jurists and originate among the jurists of the Republican era. One of our sources for Republican era jurisprudence is Cicero, who, as a pleader, frequently consulted the jurists. Cicero, beautifully capturing the jurists's distinction between the body of law (ius) and a statute (lex) as one source of law, says: "Customary law (ius) is thought to be that law which antiquity has approved by the will of all men, apart from any statute (lex)."[72] The Romans, of course, are famous for their praise of what is traditional, long standing, and ancestral: for them custom enjoyed the presumption of innocence. Moreover, Roman lawyers based their analysis of the validity of contracts and quasi-contracts on the notion of consent, both express and implied. Indeed, almost all legal obligations were treated by Roman lawyers in terms of express and implied agreements, so it was natural for them to describe the duties arising from custom in terms of a tacit or implied consent. Just as the Roman lawyers argued that contracts based on duress, fraud, or mistake were void for lack of genuine consent, so Suárez will argue that customs based on coercion or fear have no legal force.

Aristotle, by contrast, does not attempt to justify custom in terms of consent. Indeed, compared to the Roman law tradition and its scholastic

---

69. That customs must be voluntary (DL 7, 12.1): "per actus ignorantia et errore factos non inducitur consuetudo" (DL 7, 12.2); "consuetudo non inducitur per actus vi vel metu gravi factos..." (DL 7, 12.10).

70. "nam quid interest suffragio populus voluntatem suam declaret an rebus ipsis et factis?" (Digest 1.3.32). In Suárez, DL 7, 14.8.

71. For "consuetudo" as the "tacita civium conventio" (Digest 1.3.35).

72. "Consuetudine autem ius esse putatur id, quod voluntate omnium sine lege vetustas comprobarit." Cicero, *De Inventione*, II, 22.67.

commentary, Aristotle takes a rather dim view of custom. In the *Politics*, Aristotle says that moral and legal progress is evident "by the fact that old customs are exceedingly simple and barbarous" (1286b 37).[73] He goes on to say, "men in general desire the good, and not merely what their fathers had" (1269a 3). True, he also says that "customary laws have more weight, and relate to more important matters than written laws…" (*Politics*, 1287b 5), but the weight and strength of custom may stem more from blind habit than from rational consent. He says that " the force of custom is shown by the laws, in whose case, with regard to the legendary and childish elements in them, habit as more influence than our knowledge about them" (*Metaphysics* 995a 3). Aristotle puts custom before the bar of rational morality: customs are good or bad depending upon whether they are conducive or not to the common good of the citizens. The question whether customs manifest the consent of the citizens is not, for him, directly relevant to the assessment of their moral worth. He recognizes that law depends upon the support of custom and that good legislators will seek to create a harmony between law and custom. Nor does Aristotle suggest that law can transform custom; as a practical matter, even many bad customs may have to be tolerated. But he does carefully distinguish the question of the existence and longevity of a custom from the question of its righteousness. He says, for example, that many people accept the justice of slavery in accordance with the custom of war; but Aristotle then asks: "what if the cause of the war is unjust?" (*Politics* 1255a 22).

Nonetheless, there are a couple elements of Aristotle's account of custom that will enable his scholastic commentators to reconcile his views with those found in Roman law. Aristotle does say that when activities become habitual they become pleasant; and thus customs, resting as they do upon habit, could become pleasant over time. Does the pleasure we take in some customary activities manifest our consent to them? Aristotle is actually more ambivalent about the relation of habit to pleasure than his scholastic commentators. He asks, for example: "Why is it that the same things seem pleasant when we are becoming accustomed to them and not pleasant if we partake of them too continuously?" (*Problems* 928b 23).[74] Aristotle also argues that whereas laws are imposed from above, customs grow up spontaneously from below: "written laws depend on force while unwritten ones do not" (*Rhetoric* 1375a 17). Actually, of course, quite a bit

---

73. In this paragraph and the next, I have adopted the translations found in Jonathan Barnes, *The Collected Works of Aristotle* (Princeton: Princeton University Press, 1984).

74. For example, Aquinas says, "Familiar things can give us pleasure insofar as they become natural: nam consuetudo est quasi altera natura" ST I–II, 32.2 ad 3.

of social pressure is regularly applied to enforce conformity to customs, but Aristotle is right that the most obvious, direct, and violent forms of coercion are reserved for enforcement of law. Does the fact that we acquire many of our customs unreflectively and spontaneously suggest that we have consented to those customs?

Thomas Aquinas, of course, pioneered the effort of reconciling Aristotle and Roman law. Aquinas follows Aristotle in subjecting custom to objective moral standards. Thus, he says that no custom can achieve the force of law against divine and natural law: but Aquinas sounds more like Suárez here when he also says that the reason that custom cannot prevail against natural or divine law is that the divine will is superior to the human will.[75] Here we already see the presumption that custom proceeds from the will of men. Aquinas also goes even further than the Roman lawyers when he argues that custom is even a better sign of the will of the people than is a verbal declaration: "what we inwardly mean and want is most effectively declared by what outwardly and repeatedly we do."[76] Aquinas also follows the Roman lawyers in arguing that supreme lawmaking authority originally rests with the whole body of citizens, but that those citizens can transfer, even irrevocably, their legislative powers to a prince. Thus, he says that in a free city where the people retain their original lawmaking power, a popular custom expresses the legislative will of the people; but where the people have transferred their legislative power to a prince and if that prince were to tolerate a popular custom, we can assume that he approves it.[77] So custom consistent with natural and divine law becomes valid law when either democratic citizens practice it or when nondemocratic subjects practice a custom that is also tolerated by the rulers. Sheer practice of a custom signifies the consent of the people while toleration of a custom by rulers who could change it signifies their consent. Whatever the prince permits, he commands. As we shall see, both of these inferences to consent

75. "lex naturalis et divina procedit a voluntate divina, ut dictum est, unde non potest mutari per consuetudinem procedentem a voluntatis hominis... nulla consuetudo vim legis obtinere potest contra legem divinam vel legem naturalem" (ST I–II, 97.3 ad 1).

76. Aquinas goes on: "Cum enim aliquid multoties fit videtur ex deliberato rationis judicio provenire" (ST, I–II, 97.3c).

77. "Si enim sit libera multitudo, quae possit sibi legem facere, plus est consensus totius multitudinis ad aliquid observandum, quem consuetudo manifestat, quam auctoritas principis, qui non habet potestatem condendi legem, nisi inquantum gerit personam multitudinis. Unde licet singulae personae non possint condere legem, tamen totus populus legem condere potest. Si vero multitudo non habeat liberam potestatem condendi sibi legem, vel legem a superiori potestate positam removendi; tamen ipsa consuetudo in tali multitudine praevalens obtinet vim legis, inquantum per eos toleratur ad quos pertinet multitudini legem imponere, ex hoc enim ipso videntur approbare quod consuetudo induxit." ST, I–II, 97.3 ad 3.

are rash: there are many reasons to practice a custom besides consenting to it, just as there are many reasons for a prince to tolerate a custom besides approving it. Indeed, Thomas himself elsewhere in his treatise on laws explicitly rejects the view that whatever the prince permits, he commands. He argues that law cannot repress all vices, so many vices will have to be tolerated by the rulers, but that toleration is consistent with resolute disapproval (ST I–II, 99.2 ad 2). Suárez's vast exploration of customary law is a series of commentaries and footnotes on these two kinds of consent in Aquinas's discussion of custom. Suárez discusses a wide range of criteria for determining whether a usage rises to the level of a legal custom: how do we know that a usage enjoys the consent of both the people and the prince? Although Suárez places enormous weight, in principle, upon the consent of the people and of the prince, at decisive moments in the argument, he concedes that proof of consent is impossible, so that jurists may simply have to make prudential judgments about which customs to enforce as law. This reliance on concrete practical reasoning brings Suárez's account back to Aristotle's and Aquinas's emphasis on assessing the legal force of custom in relation to the objective requirements of the common good. Suárez's voluntarism turns out to provide little concrete guidance to jurists who must decide which customs merit enforcement as law.

The first challenge that Suárez faces in demonstrating that custom can be law, is in his assertion that all human law is properly found only in a perfect community, that is, an independent polity.[78] Yet on his own account, custom has full legal force in imperfect communities: the customary ius gentium is law for the community of nations while local customs are law for communities ranging in size from a nunnery to a nation.[79] Far from being restricted to a perfect community, customary law finds its natural home in imperfect communities: both the supranational community of nations and the subnational local communities. Yet according to Suárez's political theory, only a perfect community possesses by natural right the power to make law. No mere aggregation of men possesses the power to make law, only what he calls a "corpus mysticum," that is, a "corpus

78. "leges humanas habere proprie locum in quacumque communitate perfecta, non tamen in imperfecta...quia omnis communitas perfecta est proprium corpus politicum, et gubernatum per propriam jurisdictionem habentem vim coactivam, quae est legum lativa" (DL 1, 6.21).

79. Ius gentium is customary: "praecepta juris gentium in hoc different a praeceptis juris civilis, quia non scripto, sed moribus non unius vel alterius civitatis aut provinciae, sed omnium vel fere omnium nationum, constat..." (DL 2, 19.6). Iura gentium are introduced "traditione et consuetudine" rather than "constitutione" (DL 3, 2.6). Local customs, in a community of merchants or a community of nuns, may also have legal force (DL 7, 9.6, 9.8, 9.11).

politicum" (DL 3, 2.4). Not only does Suárez deny that the community of nations is a perfect community, he denies that it could ever be: he says that mankind as a whole has no legislative power and never will.[80] Suárez sees the prima facie inconsistency between his assertion that only a perfect community possesses legislative power and his assertion that ius gentium is valid human law. But he says that there is no contradiction because, even though mankind is not unified into a perfect community, the many polities need to aid each other and to cooperate in establishing justice and peace. Respecting common laws is necessary for achieving these rational goals of international society.[81] As for subnational communities, he says that they may adopt legal customs even if they are not perfect communities, but "sufficiently perfect" that true law may be imposed on them.[82] Once Suárez speaks of local communities as "sufficiently perfect," we know he is in trouble: the concept of perfect does not admit of degree. I think it fair to say that Suárez's account of the legal force of custom simply cannot be squared with his commitment to the notion of a perfect community. His attempt to reconcile these principles reveals the absence of a general theory of custom, applying both to international and subnational custom. Instead, he offers two ad hoc and seemingly unrelated accounts of these customs: international customs, he says can be lawful because the community of nations requires a stable scheme of cooperation; local communities, by contrast, possess the capacity to receive law, even if they lack the capacity to make law. There seems to be no good reason why these accounts could not be reversed, so that the community of nations has only the capacity only to receive law and local communities need stable schemes of cooperation. What does the capacity to receive law have to do with the capacity to make law? Perhaps Suárez is here referring to his claim that all valid law involves reciprocity between a prince and his people: even statutes, he says, must be received, that is, receive the consent of the people (DL 7, 18.2). By not receiving a law (perhaps ignoring it), the people possess a tacit veto power over all new law. But this reciprocity between law-makers and law-takers would seem to apply to the

---

80. "quia potestas [legislativa] haec non est in tota hominum communitate, quia non omnes component unam rempublicam aut regnum...ergo, secundum humanae naturae cursum nulla est, nec fuit, nec moraliter esse potuit potestas legislativa humana universalis pro toto orbe" (DL 3, 4.7).

81. "nam licet universalitas hominum non fuerit congregata in unum corpus politicum, sed in varias communitates divisa fuerit; nihilominus ut illae communitates sese mutuo juvare, et inter se in justitia et pace conservari possent..." (DL 3, 2.6).

82. "dicendum est consuetudinem juris non a quacumque communitate introduci posse, sed ab illa quae sit capax potestatis legislativae pro seipsa, vel saltem sufficiens, ut vera lex illi possit imponi" (DL 7, 9.6); "sufficit ergo quod sit communitas capax legis..." (DL 7, 9.11).

supranational jus gentium as much as to subnational communities. Suárez should have said that customary law can arise wherever we find stable patterns of social cooperation.

Suárez's attempt to understand all human law on the model of civil law in a perfect community undermines the generality of his account of custom. Because the civil law of one polity is not binding on residents of other polities, Suárez claims by analogy that the customs of one community are not binding on other communities.[83] But this rule applies only to local communities and not to the customs of ius gentium. Civil legislation can be regarded as reflecting the consent of the supreme political authority, but what about the customs of ius gentium? If all law manifests the will and consent of the lawgiver, then so must ius gentium. But Suárez can't seem to decide whether ius gentium rests upon consent or not. In one place, he says that ius gentium emerged by gradual trial and error, by example and imitation and not by any special agreement or consensus among peoples;[84] but in another place, he says that the community of peoples introduced common laws as if in accordance with a common pact and mutual agreement.[85] He never says of the ius gentium what he frequently says about local customs: that they express the tacit will of the people and the tacit consent of the prince.

Do We Consent to Our Customs?

We saw that Aristotle and Aquinas distinguish within custom the natural element of habit from the cultural element of convention. Habit is a kind of second nature while conventions are an unwritten law. Suárez, by contrast, divides all human customs into mutually exclusive kinds: pure custom of fact and custom of law (DL 7, 1.5 and 1.7). A custom of fact has a physical effect, namely, a habit, while a custom of law has a moral effect (DL 7, 1.4). All customs of law are also customs of fact but no mere custom of fact is also a custom of law. The only connection between fact and law in a custom is the will of the person practicing that custom. A custom of fact can become of custom of law only if the people who practice it do so with the intention of creating a legal obligation. What makes this a qualified

83. "Generalis enim regula est, ut consuetudo unius communitatis non obligat aliam distinctam" (DL, 7, 16.11).

84. "in universo introduci paulatim, et per successionem, propagationem et imitationem mutuam populorum, sine speciali conventu vel consensus omnium popularum uno tempore facto" (DL 2, 20.1).

85. "communia jura quasi communi foedere et consensione inter se observarent..." (DL 3, 2.6).

voluntarism is the fact that only some kinds of customs of fact are eligible to become customs of law: evil customs, he says, are all merely customs of fact; only morally justified customs of fact might become customs of law.[86] The closest that Suárez gets to a formal definition of a custom of law thus includes both factual habit and lawful convention: "a legitimate repetition of acts in conformity to some law or in fulfilling all the requisites of law."[87] As we shall see, the requisites of customary law include the consent of the people alone or of the people and the prince.[88]

Suárez sometimes emphasizes the priority of the consent of the people and sometimes the priority of the consent of the prince. Sometimes he defines the essence of custom in terms of the consent of the people.[89] Other times he defines the essence of custom in terms of the consent of the prince.[90] Perhaps the question of whose consent is most important depends upon the regime: Suárez says that in a democratic regime, the consent of the people alone is sufficient, but in a principate, the consent of both the people and of the prince is necessary (DL 7, 3.10). But at a deeper level, in every regime the consent of the people seems to be logically prior, in the sense that unless the people first practice a custom, thereby signaling their consent, there is nothing for the prince to consent to. The consent of the people sets the stage for the toleration or suppression of a custom by the prince.[91] The consent of the prince has no bearing unless and until the consent of the people is manifest.[92] The logical priority of the consent of the people makes customary law seem uniquely democratic: even in a polity in which the people have irrevocably alienated their lawmaking powers to a prince, customary law must still originate among the people. Suárez is aware of a problem here: if the people can transfer their lawmaking power to a prince, then why do they retain their power of making customary law? Custom seems disturbingly anomalous: princes and prelates hold unilateral power to impose all kinds of human law except customary law. With

86. "nam vitiosa consuetudo nullum jus confert" (DL 7, 1.5).

87. "esse legitimam frequentiam actuum juri alicui consentaneam, vel habentem conditiones omnes jure requisites..." (DL 7, 1.5).

88. "necessarius est consensus populi vel principis..." (DL 7, 1.12).

89. "substantiale et essentiale consuetudini, scilicet, ut sit communi populi consensus recepta." (DL 7, 2.1).

90. "Princeps vero est praecipua causa juris consuetudinis" (DL 7, 9.2).

91. "quia populus consentit, et tacite postulat consensus principis, ideo censetur princeps tacite consentire, suppositis aliis conditionibus..." (DL 7, 9.12).

92. "licet voluntas principis vel Praelati in hoc negotio sit praecipua, nihilominus magis quodammodo pendet ex voluntate populi, quia illi se accommodat (ut sic dicam) princeps, quasi licentiam concedens, ut jus consuetudinis introducat, prout voluerit, vel tanquam approbans et confirmans quod populus intendit" (DL 7, 14.5).

respect to statutory law, princes both propose and dispose laws at will; but with respect to customary law, the people propose and the prince can only accept or reject. I think it fair to say that Suárez cannot maintain both that custom is just like other kinds of human law, except unwritten (DL 7, 9.1 and 16.1) and that a body politic can alienate its lawmaking power to a prince (DL 3, 4.11). Suárez could defend his theory of the translation of legislative power to a prince by strongly distinguishing customary law from statutory law and conceding that the people cannot logically alienate their power of introducing customary law; or Suárez can defend his theory of the unity of human law by giving up the thesis that the people ever really alienate their lawmaking power. Suárez seems to subordinate his theory of the translation of lawmaking power to his theory of the unity of human law: he argues that even statutory law cannot be unilaterally imposed by princes and prelates. He says that statutes are not imposed unilaterally by princes, but that every enactment of both civil and canon law contains a tacit proviso that valid law rests upon the consent of the people.[93] Suárez's view that even statutory law rests upon the consent of the people helps to explain his assertion that statutes can be repealed by falling into desuetude (DL 7, 18.2). If, then, all human law is fundamentally the same, then the people cannot actually transfer all legislative power to a prince; all law, statutory and customary, turns out to depend upon cooperation between the people and the prince. The people can transfer the power of proposing statutes to a prince, but the people retain the power to dispose.

Consent is an interior act of the will: how do we know whether the people or the prince has consented to a custom? Consent can mean many things, ranging from a disapproving acquiescence or toleration to wholehearted affirmation and endorsement. According to Suárez, there are two aspects to consent of customary law: the material consent to the content of the custom and a legal consent to the lawful enforcement of the custom. For law to arise from custom, he says, the people must not only consent to the content of the custom but also intend that the custom be legally obligatory.[94] Suárez here seems to anticipate the well-known and controversial principle of customary international law known as "opinio iuris sive necessitatis." According to this doctrine, a usage of international conduct does not become customary international law unless those who practice it

93. "dicendo has leges [civiles et canonicas] non ferri absolute, sed sub conditione tacita, si populus eas retinere velit..." (DL 7, 18.3).

94. "non enim satis est materialiter consentire in facto sed oportet consentire in facto ut inductivo juris...quia...jus non inducitur per consuetudinem sine animo inducendi consuetudinem, id est, jus consuetudinis..." (DL 7, 12.5).

do so with the subjective conviction that the usage is already binding law.[95] However, Suárez's doctrine that custom must be practiced "cum intentione obligandi" or "animo legem inducendi" (DL 7, 14.7) avoids some of the paradoxes of the doctrine of customary international law. According to the doctrine of "opinio iuris," those who initiate a practice from which customary law may emerge, must do so with the false belief that it is already lawful. Suárez's view only requires those who practice customary law to intend that it be obligatory; they are not required to believe falsely that a custom of fact is already a custom of law. But the paradox of "opinio iuris" is the mirror image of Suárez's paradox of desuetude in which those who first derogate from law must do so either from ignorance or from the false belief that their conduct is already lawful before the law they violate eventually falls into disuse.[96] Suárez gives some examples of devotional practices, such as taking holy water at the door of a church or not eating breakfast before Mass, which he says are mere customs of fact, since they are not practiced with the intention of making binding law (DL 7, 14.6). So from the mere fact that people practice a custom, we cannot presume that they consent to its legal enforcement: they may consent to it only as a non-obligatory custom of fact.

Suárez's distinction between customs of fact and customs of law seems to collapse the crucial distinction between moral and legal obligation. We might consent to some customs (going to the movies on Saturday night) merely as customs of fact; we might consent to other customs, such as voting, intending them to be morally but not legally obligatory; and finally we might consent to customs (such as avoiding corporal punishment of children) intending them to be legally obligatory. Suárez's own examples of devotional practices appear to be neither customs of law nor mere customs of fact; those who practice them are likely to regard them as at least morally obligatory. These distinctions reveal the complexity and the hazards of inferring consent from any customary practice.

Once we accept a distinction between a custom of fact and a custom of law, we see that Suárez should not endorse Julian's claim that there is no important difference whether a people express its will by voting or by its conduct. In voting we explicitly affirm or reject proposals legally to

---

95. See Mendelson, Maurice. "The Subjective Element in Customary International Law" *British Year Book of International Law* 66 (1995) 194ff.

96. Of desuetude, Suárez says "recte posse ut consuetudo incipiat per actus malos, quia prohibitos per legem, et nihilominus inducat consuetudinem derogantem legi" (DL 7, 18.24). So people can rightfully cease to follow a merely positive law (but not a natural law) on the grounds that it has already fallen into desuetude.

enjoin, permit, or forbid certain specific acts. But our deeds do not distinguish between customs of fact and customs of law. An external observer could not discern whether we practice a custom intending it to be lawful or not; moreover, the same custom, such as speaking English or getting married, could be practiced by some as a custom of fact and by others as a custom of law and by still others as a moral custom. As we shall see, Suárez admits that it is not easy to assess whether an agent intends his custom to be lawful; Suárez even recommends a presumption that an observed practice express only a consent to customs of fact.[97]

Although Suárez concedes that the practice of a custom might signify two very different kinds of consent, he does insist that the sheer observance of a custom does signify, at the least, consent to that custom as fact.[98] But must conduct in conformity to a custom actually signify any kind of consent to that custom? One can imagine practicing some customs without any reflective awareness that they are customs, such as sleeping on a bed or eating with a fork or speaking our native language. Typically, we only become aware that a practice is a custom when we learn of alternative customs in other societies. To practice a custom reflectively requires that that we know that there are alternatives to our own customs. Does, then, a naïve and unreflective relation to custom signify the consent of the agent? It would seem not, since the notion of consent implies the notion of a choice among alternatives. Here we see, pace Julian, the yawning chasm between practicing a custom and voting. We can be said to consent to what we vote for because by definition a vote is a choice between alternatives; yet we learn and practice many customs without ever being aware of any alternative. The fact that we Americans depend upon foreigners, like Tocqueville or Bryce, to describe our customs reveals how unreflectively we practice them.

To the extent that this is true, I think we cannot infer any inward act of consent from sheer external conformity to custom. Moreover, there is even a deeper disanalogy between voting and practicing a custom. To consent to a practice or a proposal means that we must have preferences that are both prior and external to that practice or proposal that we bring to bear in evaluating it. In the case of voting, we arrive at the polls already equipped with our preferences; we don't acquire those preferences by means of voting. But in the case of custom, we acquire many customs prior to acquiring

---

97. Not easy to judge "dico non esse facile judicare de obligatione praecepti per consuetudinem inducta..."; presumption of consent only to custom of fact "quia generali est regula, quod in dubio nemo praesumitur velle obligari..." (DL 7, 15.13).

98. "quia de ratione consuetudinis est ut ex tacito et non expresso consensu introducatur" (DL 7, 2.2).

any preferences; indeed, we acquire many of our preferences precisely by acquiring our customs. Customs are not only things we might choose, they are also the means by which we choose. Our preferences are largely the product of our customs, so they cannot be treated as the basis for our acquiring those customs. Yet no one would suggest that our preferences expressed in voting could somehow be the product of the act of voting. Some activities, like voting and shopping, express our preferences and our consent; other activities, like acquiring customs or, in general, learning, form our preferences and inform our consent. By observing someone voting or shopping, we can make reliable inferences about their preferences; but observing someone speaking English or wearing pants may well not signify any consent to those customs.

A more disturbing thought is that the practice of a custom might often be consistent with potential or actual disapproval of it. Consider the customs of gender, class, and racial hierarchy: the social life of every human society is rife with customs of deference and subordination of inferiors to superiors, however defined. Sometimes these practices of social deference might be wholly naïve and reflect no awareness of alternatives; to that extent, they would not express actual approval or disapproval, neither consent nor dissent. But we might well infer from a counterfactual thought-experiment, that many social inferiors would disapprove of their own customs of deference if they became aware of alternatives. So their practice of these customs would be consistent with potential disapproval. Worse, we know from copious experience and testimony that many subject groups continue to practice customs of social deference even while resenting them. The motives to do so vary widely, from abject fear to a desire to curry favor. Nonetheless, since we have all conformed to some customs that we mildly resent or perhaps even strongly disapprove, we can clearly see that sheer conformity to a custom is very poor evidence of any kind of consent to it.

As we saw, Suárez is explicitly aware of the dangers of inferring consent to a custom of law from mere conformity to it. But Suárez also seems implicitly aware of the hazards of inferring any kind of consent from mere conformity. As we noted, he attempts to define custom so as to exclude the possibility of customs bring practiced without consent. A custom, he says, must be a voluntary act, meaning that agent must be the cause of the deed. An act would be nonvoluntary if the agent did not know what he was doing or was mistaken about what he was doing;[99] an act would also be

---

99. "ergo, ut consuetudinem introducant, necessarium est ut voluntarii sint" (DL 7, 12.1); "per actus ignorantia et errore factos non inducitur consuetudinem. . ." (DL 7, 12.2).

nonvoluntary if it were done by coercion or from great and unjust fear.[100] Suárez is aware that in the Aristotelian-Thomistic tradition, an act may be voluntary even if motivated by great fear (DL 7, 12.11): Aristotle's famous example is a ship captain's decision to jettison his cargo during a storm. According to Aristotle, that captain acted voluntarily. Suárez, however, sees fear as incompatible with full consent to legal custom: he says that even a frequent act done solely from fear is never a sufficient sign of the consent of a people to introduce a custom.[101] Because Suárez immediately goes on to say that we cannot presume the prince to consent to a custom based on fear, it is clear that Suárez is here discussing consent to binding legal custom, not consent to a custom of fact.

Do these stipulations defining the voluntary nature of customary conduct ensure that all customs reliably express the consent of those who practice them? A naïve and unreflective practice might be but need not be based on ignorance or error. I might not be reflectively aware that there are other languages besides English; but my use of English is not based on ignorance or error. Ignorance or error would lead me to speak the wrong language or to speak it in the wrong way based on my mistaken understanding of the relevant customs. So my deeply naïve practices might well be voluntary and yet lack any element of consent. On Suárez's account, some considerable degree of fear, falling short of serious and unjust fear, is compatible with the voluntary nature at least of customs of fact. What to say about our customs of social deference and subordination? When those customs are ruthlessly enforced by violence (say, by the KKK), Suárez would deny that conformity to such custom is a sign of any kind of consent. But most customs of social subordination are enforced by much subtler threats and incentives: if we "know what is good for us" we will show proper deference. In these more common cases in which customs may well be practiced with resentment, Suárez seems to say that we should not interpret conformity to these customs as evidence of consent to binding customary law. So the customary deference of black to white Americans in the South should not be interpreted as consent to the legal enforcement of racial customs. Yet Suárez does seem to permit the inference that, absent ruthless violence, blacks could be said to consent to the practices of racial deference as customs of fact. In short, Suárez seems unaware that there are

100. "consuetudinem non obtinere neque induci per actus factos per vim vel gravem et injuriosum metum" (DL 7, 12.10).

101. "frequentia actuum ex solo metu factorum nunquam est sufficiens signum publici consensus totius populi de consuetudine inducenda" (DL 7, 12.11).

many other motives for voluntarily conforming to custom besides consent, meaning that it is very doubtful to infer consent from the sheer fact of conformity to custom.

Among free peoples, the consent of the people to the legal force of custom is sufficient to introduce customary law; but among subjects of a prince, the consent of the people is necessary but not sufficient—the prince must also consent to the custom (DL 7, 3.10). There are several ways for a prince to consent: Suárez distinguishes personal from legal consent (DL 7, 13.6). A prince may give personal consent either expressly or tacitly (as when he is aware of the custom but does not suppress it); a prince gives legal consent when he enacts a law to enforce the custom. The tacit consent of a prince to a custom is sufficient to make it valid law (DL 7, 18.9). Just as Suárez attempted to infer the tacit consent of a people to a custom, not from their words, but from their deeds, so here he attempts to infer the tacit consent of a prince to a custom, not by what he says (either in person or in law) but by what he does. It is safe to assume that people who practice a custom have knowledge of it, even if they lack knowledge of it as a custom. But the tacit consent of the prince to a custom in no way depends upon his practice of it. Suárez says that in order to establish the tacit consent of the prince we must establish two distinct mental acts: first, he must have knowledge of the custom; second, he must approve of the custom.[102] Suárez will attempt to show at length, what circumstantial evidence might reliably indicate that the prince both has knowledge of a custom and approves it. The core claim here is that since the prince has the power to suppress any (though not all) custom, if he is aware of a custom yet does not suppress it, he must approve it. Whatever the prince permits, he commands. This argument that custom is the tacit command of the sovereign stems from the jurists of Roman law, and can be found in Aquinas, Hobbes, and John Austin.

Even assuming the prince has knowledge of a custom, Suárez is aware that the mere fact that he tolerates a custom is far from proof that he approves it. The prince may well have to tolerate patiently many things of which he does not approve.[103] Suárez does not explore the various motives that might lead a prince to tolerate customs even when he disapproves of

102. "necessarium esse consensum principis personalem, saltem tacitum, ac subinde necessarium etiam esse ut scientiam consuetudinis habeat..." (DL 7, 13.11); "Solum oportet ut moraliter constet, tolerantiam non esse tantum permissivam, sed operativam, seu approbativam..." (DL 7, 13.12).

103. "quia tolerantia sola, supposita scientia, non indicat sufficientier consensum, quia multa per patientiam tolerantur, quae non approbantur..." (DL 7, 13.12).

them. H.L.A. Hart, in his devastating critique of John Austin's use of this argument, observes that a prince might tolerate a custom he loathes because he cannot suppress it, or because it would be too costly to suppress it, or he seeks to placate a subordinate, and so on.[104] For these reasons, Suárez says that we must look to the circumstances and context of the prince's toleration to determine if he has knowledge of a custom and, if so, whether he approves it.[105] When we examine these circumstantial factors, we see that the will and consent of the prince lose much of their significance; the legal validity of custom will turn out to rest upon objective reasonableness of the custom and upon the prudential judgment of lawyers evaluating the custom. Suárez's discussion of the length of time it takes to establish a legal custom (DL 7, 15) does not consider what long or short duration mean for the objective structure of customary order in society. Aristotle and Aquinas argue that, other things equal, older customs are more entrenched in the habits of the people, and thus will become second nature. We conform to long-standing customs spontaneously and because we rely on them more, they will be harder to change. In other words, for Aristotle and Aquinas the durability of custom is a sign of the tenacity of the order of custom in human life. But Suárez discusses the duration of a custom mainly in relation to what it signifies about the knowledge and consent of the prince.[106] He says that we cannot presume the consent of the prince or of the people, unless a custom is practiced sufficiently frequently and over sufficient time.[107] According to Suárez, there is no fixed rule about how long a custom must last or how frequently it must be practiced in order to establish the knowledge and approval of the prince. Other things equal, he says, a custom practiced more frequently and over a longer period of time is more likely to be known by and approved by the prince (DL 7, 15.9).

Voluntarism Collapses into Naturalism

Ultimately, Suárez does not put much weight on these objective measures of a custom's frequency or duration: he says that even if a custom lasts for 1000 years, it has no legal force unless those who practice it do so

104. See Hart, H.L.A. *The Concept of Law* (Oxford: Clarendon Press, 1961), 43–48.

105. "tolerantiam per se non sufficere, adjunctis vero circumstantis posse esse prudens et morale signum" (DL 7, 18.20).

106. In one place, Suárez does describe durable custom as a second nature that is very difficult to change (DL 7, 20.5).

107. "tacitus consensus populi aut principis non praesumitur, nisi diuturno tempore et per sufficientem actuum frequentiam de illo constet" (DL 7, 11.14).

with the intention of creating binding law.[108] Again, by contrast to Aristotle and Aquinas, he is not interested in the objective social order created by custom but in the will and intention of the lawmakers. What visible signs reliably indicate that the people and the prince have the proper intentions that constitute consent to a custom? Suárez offers some criteria for determining when a custom is likely to signify the consent of the people and prince (DL 7, 15.13). First, if the custom is durable and deals with serious and difficult conduct, onerous matters, and is observed by a majority of the people; second, if prudent and conscientious men think ill of those who do not observe the custom or if the people generally are scandalized by its nonobservance; third, if the governors or prelates of the republic strongly censure or punish those who do not conform; fourth, if the substance of the custom is strongly conducive to the common good of the polity and if prudent men find it very advantageous to enforce it as law. Suárez claims that these criteria reliably establish the consent of the people to introduce customary law, but if we examine these criteria we see that the work of justification of custom is not being done by the will of any lawmaker. All the heavy lifting is being done by the objective requirements of the common good and the prudential judgment of the statesmen.

In other words, despite Suárez's immense theoretical labor to establish that will is the essence of law, at the decisive moment when he offers criteria to guide jurists in the task of deciding how to interpret or whether to enforce a law, Suárez relies almost wholly on the traditional criteria of objective morality and prudential judgment. Where there is any doubt about what a legislator actually wills, we must presume that his will is rational and just. We know, he says, that God wills us to avoid all intrinsic evil. How do we know God's will? Because we must presume that He cannot be irrational or unjust.[109] These presumptions play an especially prominent role in his analysis of customary law. Suárez concedes that visible signs of the interior will are never truly reliable, so that in practice the decisions about whether to enforce custom must be left to the discretion of prudent men.[110] Similarly, in his discussion of when custom can abrogate law, Suárez turns to objective criteria rather than to the will. For example,

---

108. "nunquam enim praescribitur consuetudo ad effectum inducendi legem, etiamsi per mille annos duret, nisi frequentia actuum facta sit ex intentione inducendi jus" (DL 7, 15.10).

109. "quia voluntas Dei non potest esse irrationalibilis…" DL 2, 6.8. "quia cum haec [lex naturalis] sit vera lex, et Deum habeat auctorem, non potest non esse honestum…" DL, 2, 7.1.

110. "dico judicium de modo consuetudinis, et animo quo introducta est, arbitrio prudentium esse relinquendum…" (DL 7, 15.13); "in quo nulla certa regula assignari potest, sed prudenti arbitrio relinquendum est" (DL 7, 17.2).

if an evil custom of the people is tolerated by the prince, we must not infer that he has tacitly approved it, "since an evil will is not to be presumed of the prince."[111] Conversely, if a good custom of the people threatens to abrogate a bad statute, then the toleration of a prince is properly interpreted as a sign of his consent, since the will of the prince is presumed to be reasonable.[112] If the will of the prince is to be interpreted according to objective moral standards, then law gets its authority not only from the will of the prince but also from those standards. In his discussion of the interpretation of law, Suárez insists that all kinds of interpretation must be oriented toward discerning the will of the legislator. But since that will often cannot be reliably known, jurists must presume the legislator to be just and reasonable (DL 6, 1.17). Suárez even says that jurists should presume that a legislator intends a new law to harmonize with existing law (DL 6, 1.18).

Here we see the difficulty of deciding whether Suárez is a voluntarist or a realist. His formal account of law is voluntarist but always hedged by realist claims that valid law cannot violate natural or divine law: "lex injusta non est lex" (DL 3, 22.1). And though he argues at length that the validity of customary laws rests upon the consent of the people alone or the people and the prince, these assertions are hedged and qualified by his claims that valid custom cannot violate divine or human law (DL 7, 6.7). These appeals to natural and divine law, to the common good, and to the prudential judgment of leaders make Suárez sound like a Thomist. Yet, as we saw above, when we explore what he means by divine and natural law, we see that they trump human law, not so much because they set forth the general requirements of the common good, but largely because they signify a will higher than a human will. Suárez does not ask "what does natural or divine law mean?" but rather "what did God mean by his law?" Nonetheless, at decisive moments in his analysis of the legal force of custom, Suárez appeals to objective morality and prudential judgment. In one place, Suárez suggests how these realist appeals might be consistent with a qualified voluntarism (DL 7, 18.10): for custom or statute to become valid human law it must pass through two very different kinds of filters. First, all human law must be consistent with natural and divine law; but infinitely many human laws can meet this test, even incompatible laws within one society, so we need a second filter to select which of those myriad possible laws should be enforced. The will and consent of the lawmaker, then,

---

111. "quia non est praesumenda prava voluntas in principe" (DL, 7, 18.20); confer DL 7, 18.9.

112. " . . . ut prudens censeatur abrogatio; tunc enim merito praesumitur consensus in principe, sciente et patiente talem consuetudinem" (DL 7, 18.20).

selects among the set of laws consistent with higher law.[113] To be consistent with natural and divine law is necessary but not sufficient for valid human law: only law that is both consistent with higher law and reflects the will and consent of the lawmakers is valid law.

This argument about two filters works only if the two filters are independent of each other. But we have seen that Suárez often concedes that we have no reliable way to interpret the will of a lawmaker, so we must presume his will to be just, reasonable, and conducive to the common good. But these presumptions reveal that the actual will of the lawmaker is often superfluous. What matters for the basic justification of law is not whether people actually do consent to a law but whether they ought to consent to it. In relation to a different question, the question of the efficacy of law, we might want to know if the people will consent to it. If even a morally good law totally lacks popular consent, then it will fail or even backfire in its enforcement and effects. So some degree of consent may well be necessary for law to be effective, but what matters for the basic justification of law is that people ought to consent to it because it is morally and practically sound. We see the same shift from an actual to a merely presumed will in arguments that we ought to interpret a statute in light of the will or intention of the legislator. When circumstances arise in the application of that statute, as they usually do, not foreseen by the original lawmakers, then we must ask, not what did they intend, but what would they have intended. The only sound way to presume a hypothetical will is to appeal to objective morality and the judgment of prudent leaders. What this means is that although Suárez champions a basically voluntarist theory of law, in practice the actual will of the lawmaker often cannot be reliably known. When that is the case, Suárez counsels recourse to natural law and legislative prudence, just like his teacher, Thomas Aquinas.

---

113. "ergo, ut consuetudo sit rationabilis, non satis est quod non sit contra rationem naturalem, nec contra jus divinum, nec quod non sit jure reprobata, sed necessarium est, ut voluntas carendi tali lege aliqua ratione honestari posit in subditis..." (DL 7, 18.10).

CHAPTER 3 | A Commentary on the *Comment*: Jeremy Bentham's Theory of Custom

JEREMY BENTHAM IS NOTORIOUS for his verbal abuse of custom. In one famous exclamation, he accuses custom of somehow being both a tyrant and a slave: "Ah! When will the yoke of Custom—Custom, the blind tyrant which all other tyrants make their slave—ah! when will that misery-perpetuating yoke be shaken off? When, when will Reason be seated on her throne?"[1] Yet, in other places, Bentham acknowledges that custom cannot be a tyrant for the same reason that custom cannot be enslaved by a tyrant: tyrants have purposes and agendas, but custom is the unintentional by-product of human action. In this sense, custom cannot be misused because it cannot be used at all. Thus, Bentham sometimes strongly distinguishes "spontaneous" custom from compulsory or legal custom: tyrants have no power over spontaneous custom, only over law.[2] Far from advocating the wholesale abolition of custom in the name of rational reform, Bentham shows great sensitivity to the dangers of the legal reform of custom; hence, he advocates a middle ground between wholesale attack on custom and blind conformity to all customs.[3] Indeed,

---

1. Bentham, *Plan of Parliamentary Reform* (London: T. J. Wooler, 1817) 75.
2. Bentham, *A Comment on the Commentaries* [hereafter *Comment*], Eds. J. H. Burns and H.L.A. Hart (Oxford: Clarendon Press, 2008) 234–236.
3. "He who attacks prejudice wantonly and without necessity and he who suffers himself to be led blindfold a slave to it, equally miss the line of reason." Jeremy Bentham, "Essay on the Influence of Time and Place in Matters of Legislation" in *The Works of Jeremy Bentham*, Ed. John Bowring [hereafter *Works*], Vol. 1, 169–194, at 180. As Jennifer Pitts says, "Contrary to his reputation as a radical reformer indifferent to or contemptuous of custom and lived experience, Bentham insists that would-be legislators exercise great caution before presuming to interfere with existing

Bentham's cautious respect for the power of custom led him to advocate more tolerance for what he considers immoral custom than did the British rulers of India. Thus, Bentham sees no good reason to suppress the custom of sati, so long as a widow throws herself upon the funeral pyre voluntarily.[4] Bentham clearly sees that custom is more durable and often more permanent than law. For example, he rightly predicted that the fandango would outlast the existing legal institutions of Latin America.[5]

Bentham could also be inconsistent about the relation of custom to reason. In several places, he starkly contrasts custom to reason: "when will Reason be seated in her throne?" Sometimes Bentham calls custom the "law of fools" and claims that custom is merely "the offspring and servant of sinister interest."[6] However, in other places, Bentham shows a much more nuanced understanding of the relation of custom to reason: he acknowledges that reason provides no precise determination in many matters, so customary conventions ought to decide these intrinsically arbitrary matters, such as the precise age of majority. Furthermore, customary habits deserve rational respect because they often embody legitimate expectations whose disappointment is the occasion of much pain. Bentham even goes so far as to argue for the presumptive rationality of custom, shifting the burden of proof onto those who seek to abolish custom: "Custom, though not good against reason, is always good in default of reason to the contrary: failing specific and preponderant inconveniences, it is not only a reason but a conclusive one."[7] Thus, Bentham sagely concludes that "there is a custom which is reason's offspring. There is a custom which is reason's enemy…"[8] Clearly, Bentham the Enlightenment polemicist sometimes got the better of Bentham the philosopher.

---

practices." Jeremy Bentham, "Great and Distant Crimes" in *Selected Writings of Jeremy Bentham*. Ed. Stephen G. Engelmann (New Haven: Yale University Press, 2011) 478–499 at 487.

4. "An Hindoo woman every now and then takes it into her head to burn herself upon the death of her husband: if the act is altogether voluntary.… I can see no reason why she should not be indulged.…" Bentham, "Place and Time" in *Selected Writings of Jeremy Bentham* 152–219, at 174.

5. "*Customs*, which in so far as they stand clear of laws and institutions, are free, have in the nature of the case, on that account, a better chance for permanence. The *fandango*, having neither been made obligatory nor been instituted by law, might still continue in use, when every law and every institution had long been changed." Bentham in *Colonies, Commerce, and Constitutional Law*, Ed. Philip Schofield (Oxford: Clarendon Press, 1995) 119.

6. For custom as the Law of Fools, see *First Principles Preparatory to Constitutional Code*, Ed. Philip Schofield (Oxford: Clarendon Press, 1989) 115; for custom as servant of sinister interest, see *Colonies, Commerce, and Constitutional Law*, Ed. Philip Schofield, 83.

7. Bentham, *Colonies, Commerce, and Constitutional Law*, Ed. Philip Schofield, 93.

8. Of the age of majority, he says: "fixation can not be other than in a great degree arbitrary and casual. Custom may therefore be allowed to determine." As for why it is rational to respect customary habits: "By departure from custom, disappointment is produced: and, by disappointment, disquietude, uneasiness, pain." Bentham, *First Principles Preparatory to Constitutional Code* 97; on custom as reason's offspring, see 115n.

As with Aristotle, Aquinas, and Suárez, Bentham's theory of custom is explicitly grounded by him in his epistemology, ontology, logic, and philosophy of language. Indeed, as a metaphysician, Bentham is best known for his ontology of real and fictitious entities. For this reason, even though Gerald Postema chose not to ground Bentham's theory of custom explicitly in Bentham's metaphysics in his influential book, he nevertheless acknowledges the importance of Bentham's theory of fictitious entities, and he claims that his own account of custom in Bentham is "much influenced" by that theory.[9] Thus, here, I will attempt explicitly to ground Bentham's theory of custom in his theory of fictitious entities. Moreover, in contrast to Postema, I will focus here on custom rather than on customary law, because Bentham uses "customary law" exclusively to mean "common law," and Bentham's theory of common law is only very indirectly relevant to a general theory of custom. Indeed, like his teacher Blackstone, Bentham usually divides all law into statute and "custom," where custom refers only to common law.[10] Thus, Bentham uses the expressions "customary law" and "custom" to refer almost exclusively to common law. Accordingly, Bentham almost always thinks of custom as "legalized custom"—that is, as custom recognized by courts of law. Indeed, when speaking of informal social practices, Bentham is more likely to call them "habits" than customs.[11] So Bentham leaves little conceptual or lexical space between habit and law—yet true custom lives precisely in that space.

Bentham's Theory of Fictitious Entities

What is most distinctive of Bentham's theory of custom is his doctrine that custom is a fictitious entity. We are thus drawn ineluctably, though perhaps reluctantly, into Bentham's general theory of fictitious entities—a theory with ontological, epistemological, linguistic, literary, legal, moral, and political dimensions. Throughout his writings, Bentham makes innumerable claims that familiar words in philosophical, legal, and popular discourse are names of fictitious entities. In addition to the legal fictions

---

9. Postema, *Bentham and the Common Law Tradition* (Oxford: Clarendon Press, 1986) 296.

10. "Laws may exist in the form of statutes or in the form of customs. The statute law is called written positive law; custom is a conjectural law which is drawn by induction from the former decisions given by the judges in similar cases." Bentham, "General View of a Complete Code of Laws," in *Works*, Vol. 3, 155–210, at 157.

11. Thus Bentham contrasts the customs of southern and northern England in terms of a "habit of idleness" and a "habit of industry." See *Writings on the Poor Laws*, Vol. 1, Ed. Michael Quinn (Oxford: Clarendon Press, 2001) 17 and 45. But, as noted above, Bentham does sometimes refer to informal social practices (such as the fandango) as a custom.

familiar to lawyers, Bentham also claims that the doctrines of a social contract or of tacit consent are fictions; and, more troubling, he asserts that familiar concepts such as common law, society, mankind, nature, redness, mind, and rights are names of fictitious entities. Bentham also has a theory of legal and political fictions, but these should not be confused with his theory of fictitious entities.[12] Novices to Bentham's metaphysics will be surprised to learn that although utility, motion, space, and time are fictitious, Bentham insists that God and his angels are real.[13]

How original is Bentham's analysis of fictitious and real entities? Philip Schofield cites Hart's authority for the claim that "Bentham's analysis of real and fictitious entities was one of his most original contributions to the history of philosophy." But in the referenced passage, Hart says that Bentham's greatest originality lay elsewhere.[14] Speaking *propria voce*, Schofield goes even further to assert that Bentham's doctrine of fictitious entities "was, perhaps, as original an idea as any philosopher has produced."[15] Yet, what are regarded as striking innovations in modern philosophy often turn out to be merely recycled scholasticism. In fact, Bentham's distinction between real and fictitious entities was a commonplace of scholastic logic and metaphysics. The basic scholastic distinction was between mind-independent being (*ens reale*) and mind-dependent being (*ens rationis*). Language treats even figments of the imagination on the model (*ad instar*) of mind-independent beings: we talk about golden mountains and unicorns as if they really existed. As Bentham says: "When

---

12. Schofield rightly warns us: "The use of the phrase 'theory of fictions' to refer to Bentham's thinking on ontology, logic, language, and grammar, though common in the secondary literature, is potentially confusing. Bentham did very occasionally use the term 'fiction' to represent what he meant by the term 'fictitious entity,' but the two terms normally referred to distinct, albeit related ideas.... Hence, it appears to be more accurate, as well as less confusing, when discussing Bentham's ontology, to speak of his theory of real and fictitious entities, rather than of his theory of fictions." Philip Schofield, *Utility and Democracy* (Oxford: Oxford University Press, 2006) 2n.

13. Bentham frequently describes spiritual entities such as God, angels and the soul, as "inferential real entities." If this sounds less than fully real, we should note that Bentham refers to all corporeal bodies as "inferential real entities" since the only entities that we perceive directly are sensations, impressions, and ideas. See Bentham, "Ontology," in *Works*, Vol. 8, 192–211 at 196.

14. Here is what Hart actually says: "Bentham's best-known contribution to logic and linguistic theory is his doctrine of Logical Fictions.... However, the most original of Bentham's contributions to logic is his form of imperative or deontic logic which he calls the Logic of the Will." Hart, H.L.A. *Essays on Bentham: Studies in Jurisprudence and Political Theory* (Oxford Oxfordshire: Clarendon, 1982) 11–12. Schofield makes his claim about Hart in "Political and Religious Radicalism in the Thought of Jeremy Bentham" *History of Political Thought* 20/2 (Summer 1999) 272–291 at 291.

15. Schofield, *Bentham: A Guide for the Perplexed* (London: Continuum 2009) 17. In person, Schofield says that Bentham's originality lay not so much in the distinction of real and fictitious entities but in Bentham's methods for reducing fictitious to real entities.

spoken of, mental ideas are spoken of as if they were corporeal ones. In no other manner can they be spoken of."[16] Within mind-dependent being, various scholastics made further distinctions: some mind-dependent beings were thought to have a foundation in reality, such as, for realists, logical universals and relations; other mind-dependent beings were thought to have no foundation in reality, such as goat-stags and chimeras.[17] But many nominalists, like Bentham, treated all logical universals as mere constructs (*entia ficta*). Henry of Harclay, chancellor of Oxford University (1313–1316), is usually credited with being the first to argue that all universals are *ficta*; William of Ockham seems to have derived his *fictum* theory from Harclay, his teacher. Just as Harclay verbally distinguished logical fictions (*ficta*) from poetical fictions (*figmenta*), so Bentham verbally distinguished the "fictitious entities" of logic from the "fabulous entities" of the poets.[18] Bentham could also have found his notion of "fictitious entities" in the work of that later student of Oxford scholasticism, Thomas Hobbes.[19] Bentham thus appears to be heir to an ancient tradition of nominalist metaphysics based in Oxford. Moreover, it is worth noting that Bentham himself claimed no great originality for his "fictitious entities" and instead, attributes both the idea and expression to D'Alembert.[20]

Virtually no one accuses Bentham of being a great metaphysician, and despite the efforts of some major analytic philosophers, no one has yet found a coherent theory of Bentham's celebrated distinction between real and fictitious entities.[21] Postema rightly says: "The principle of distinction underlying this classification is never made fully explicit and never defended

---

16. Bentham, "Essay on Language," in *Works*, Vol. 8: 294–338 at 327.

17. John of St. Thomas (John Poinsot), an Iberian scholastic of the 17th century, provides a good overview of the debates: he says that almost everyone agrees on the distinction between truly mind-independent being (*ens reale*) and purely imaginary or impossible beings (*entia ficta*). See John Poinsot, *Tractatus de Signis*, ed. John Deely (Berkeley: University of California Press, 1985) 48–49.

18. For Harclay, see Stephan Read, "The Objective Being of Ockham's *Ficta*" in *The Philosophical Quarterly* 27/106 (Jan. 1977), 14–31 at 24; and Maurer, Armand A. *The Philosophy of William of Ockham in Light of its First Principles* (Toronto: Pontifical Institute of Medieval Studies, 1999) 505; for Bentham, see "Ontology," 199.

19. Hobbes distinguishes real from fictive entities (*ficta*) in his *Computatio sive Logica*, bi-lingual edition trans. by Aloysius Martinich, eds. Isabel Hungerland and George Vick (New York: Abaris Books, 1981) Chap. 2, Par. 6: 202.

20. "D'Alembert is the author in whose works the notion of this distinction was first observed by me:—*être fictif* is the expression employed by him for the designation of the sort of object for the designation of which the appellation *fictitious entity* has ever since been employed." Bentham, "Logical Arrangements," in *Works*, Vol. 3, 285–295, at 286. Bentham also credits D'Alembert for the distinction between the names of real and fictitious entities in *Chrestomathia,* Eds. M. J. Smith and W. H. Burston (Oxford: Clarendon Press, 1983): 257.

21. For valiant attempts, see John Wisdom, *Interpretation and Analysis* (London: Kegan Paul, 1931) and the critique of Wisdom in C. K. Ogden, *Bentham's Theory of Fictions* (London: Kegan Paul, 1932).

by Bentham."[22] Bentham presents his distinction in many different places, and these presentations are not mutually consistent. Schofield attempts to reconstruct Bentham's doctrine to show that real entities must be physical objects: "A real entity was a 'corporeal substance'—an object which really had existence…"[23] But Bentham explicitly and repeatedly insists that real entities include "incorporeal substances."[24] Moreover, Bentham often divides the class of "real entities" into physical and psychical; among the real psychical entities he lists ideas, impressions, and sensations, including the sensations of pain and pleasure.[25] These psychical real entities cannot be themselves physical entities. Can we reduce psychical entities to physical ones? If we could, then the psychical entities would be fictitious, for a fictitious entity, by contrast to a fabulous one, is an entity that can be reduced to a real one. But Bentham claims that psychical entities are real; therefore, they cannot be reduced to physical entities. In short, whatever makes psychical entities real cannot be the same thing that makes physical entities real. Far from reducing psychical real entities to physical ones, Bentham often argues that psychical entities alone are perceptible, while physical entities are merely inferential.[26]

If Bentham's physicalist ontology is foundational, and if, as Schofield says, "Bentham's epistemology was founded upon his ontology," then we would expect physical objects to be what is most knowable.[27] Yet Bentham notoriously argues that sensations, impressions, and ideas are the only direct objects of knowledge since the only things we know for certain are the percepts and concepts of our own minds—our knowledge of physical objects is indirect, inferential, and uncertain.[28] So Bentham's Lockean epistemology is clearly not founded upon a physicalist ontology, even though it may be compatible with it. Ideas and sensations could

---

22. See Postema, "Facts, Fictions, and Law," in *Facts in Law*, Ed. William Twining (Wiesbaden: Franz Steiner, 1983) 37–64 at 47.
23. Schofield, "Political and Religious Radicalism in the Thought of Jeremy Bentham," 277.
24. Bentham says that "incorporeal substances" are "inferential real entities" in "Ontology," 196–197 and in *Chrestomathia*: 271n. True, as Schofield points out, Bentham argues that our inferences to corporeal entities "are stronger, more necessary, and more irresistible" than our inferences to incorporeal entities. See "Ontology," 197.
25. Bentham, "Essay on Logic," 265 and 247.
26. "entities are either real or fictitious: real, either *perceptible* or *inferential*: perceptible, either *impressions* or *ideas*: inferential, either material, i.e. *corporeal* or *immaterial*, i.e. spiritual." Here we can see that corporeal and incorporeal entities are equally inferential. See Bentham, *Chestomathia*, 271n.
27. See Schofield, "Political and Religious Radicalism in the Thought of Jeremy Bentham," 277.
28. "Speaking of Entities, ideas might perhaps accordingly be spoken of as the *sole perceptible ones*…" Bentham, "Ontology," 196. As Schofield observes: "Even knowledge of the physical world is problematic to the extent that the human mind does not perceive that world directly, but rather its perceptions of that world." *Bentham: A Guide for the Perplexed* 51.

be first in knowledge even if physical substances are first in being. But Bentham notoriously calls both corporeal and non-corporeal entities real, so his ontology is not simply physicalist. Moreover, Bentham, as Schofield says, does want his epistemology to be founded upon his ontology: he wants what is most real also to be what is most knowable. Bentham has no treatise on epistemology and in his ontology he implicitly treats Locke's sensationalism as an ontology of phenomenalism: ideas and sensations are not only first in knowledge but also first in being.

How does Locke's epistemological sensationalism lead to ontological phenomenalism? Before addressing that question, I will here observe only that since we have ideas of both corporeal and non-corporeal entities, ontological phenomenalism can explain how Bentham can include both corporeal and non-corporeal entities in his category of real entities. Yet, as Schofield rightly says, Bentham also sometimes attempts to reduce non-corporeal entities to corporeal ones, suggesting a physicalist ontology. His materialism leads him to treat physical entities as foundational while his Lockean sensationalism leads him to treat ideas and impressions as foundational. To this unresolved war between Bentham's ontological materialism and his ontological phenomenalism, we must add a third belligerent, Bentham's metaphysical nominalism. As a nominalist, he tries to make individual persons or things foundational: "strictly speaking, *individual* objects are the only real entities" (*Chrestomatic* 258n) and "names of real entities are masses of proper names." But pleasure and pain are not individual things with proper names, yet he makes pleasure and pain foundational real entities.[29] In short, Bentham's nominalism, his materialism, and his phenomenalism pull him and his theory of real and fictitious entities in mutually inconsistent directions. We shall see how his nominalism, materialism, and phenomenalism shape his theory of custom and law.

The best way to understand Bentham's logic and linguistics is against an Aristotelian background. Aristotle says famously in *On Interpretation* (*Peri hermeneias*): "spoken words are symbols of the passions of the soul" and "passions of the soul are likenesses of real things" (16a 3–8). Aristotle's commentators developed this cryptic remark into a profound theory of signs that unified language and cognition. In the medieval semiotic, written and spoken words were called "instrumental signs" because they had to be first cognized as objects before they could signify; by contrast, percepts and concepts of the mind were called "formal signs" because they

---

29. See Bentham, "Essay on Logic," in *Works*, Vol. 8: 213–293 at 247. On why pleasure and pain are not individual things, see Wisdom, *Interpretation and Analysis* 132–133.

refer the mind to objects without having to be first cognized as objects. Of course, percepts and concepts could also be treated as objects of reflection or what they called "second intentions." This semiotic theory was the basis for metaphysical realism: words were said to refer directly to objects by means of percepts and concepts. Fundamentally, we do not cognize our percepts and concepts; rather, we cognize the world by means of percepts and concepts. In this view, our sensations and ideas are not pictures of the world, they are not mental objects; instead, they are windows or lenses through which we know the world. Modern philosophy, both Cartesian rationalism and Lockean empiricism, treats sensations and ideas, not as signs of the world but as mental objects, as an internal sensorium or mental theater of representations. Of course, once we erect this world of internal, mental objects the question immediately arises about the relationship of this mental theater to the external world.

Thus, both modern idealism and empiricism generate deep skepticism about the reality of objects beyond the mental impressions and ideas that we know.[30] Bentham often voices this deep skepticism, as when he says "speaking of Entities, ideas might perhaps accordingly be spoken of as the *sole perceptible ones*; substances, those of the corporeal class, being, with reference, and in contradistinction to them, no other than *inferential ones*." Thus, compared to the certainty of our direct knowledge of ideas, our knowledge of corporeal bodies is remote and indirect; but compared to our knowledge of incorporeal bodies, Bentham says that our knowledge of corporeal bodies is direct and certain.[31] As Ross Harrison says, "like Hume or Locke before him, what we now think of as mental states are regarded as individual objects or entities."[32] We see further evidence of Bentham's skepticism in his definition of language: "Language is the sign of thought, of the thought which is in the mind of him by whom the discourse is uttered." Returning to the Aristotelian semiotic: Bentham defines language as a sign of thought; but he never defines impressions or ideas as signs of external objects. Like the other classic modern philosophers, Bentham has no unified semiotic of language and thought, because the contents of our thought (impressions or ideas) are not signs but objects.

30. For a discussion of the scholastic doctrine of the instrumental and formal sign, see James B. Murphy, "Nature, Custom, and Stipulation in the Semiotic of John Poinsot," *Semiotica* 83 (1/2) 1991: 33–68.

31. Bentham, "Ontology," 196–197.

32. Harrison, *Bentham* (London: Routledge and Kegan Paul, 1983) 56. Harrison denies that Bentham's treatment of ideas as objects of cognition leads him to any real skepticism: "Bentham has no problem in thinking of perception in terms of our awareness of the physical world." (55). Yet Bentham repeatedly asserts that we perceive only ideas directly.

True, Bentham does not deny that language can refer to the world in addition to referring to thought: "It [language] may be the sign of other things and other objects in infinite variety, but of this object [thought] it is always a sign, and it is only through this that it becomes the sign of any other object."[33] So, language may also be a sign of objects in the world, but all we can be certain of is that language is a sign of thought.[34]

We are now in a position to see why Postema's proposal for making Bentham's doctrine coherent creates more problems than it solves. Postema offers this interpretation for Bentham's distinction between real and fictitious entities: "The principle that seems to be at work most often in Bentham's discussion rests on a notion of dependence and independence: fictitious entities are dependent on other entities (real or ficititious), whereas real entities are independent and self-sufficient."[35] This principle poses a dilemma for Bentham: either he surrenders his view that ideas are real entities so that they can become dependent upon real entities (as in, for example, physicalism) or he affirms that ideas are independent and self-sufficient real entities at the cost of denying that there are any other real entities (as in, for example, Berkeleyan phenomenalism). Either horn of this dilemma is fatal to his basic doctrine: physicalism prevents pleasure and pain from being real while phenomenalism prevents corporeal substances from being real. Here we see how Bentham's physicalism (the mental is derivative of the physical) is at war with his phenomenalism (physical bodies are derivative of our ideas of them).

Customary Law as Fiction

Since Bentham claims that the word "law" is the name of a fictitious entity, it is not surprising that he also asserts frequently that "the customary [i.e. common] law is a fiction from beginning to end."[36] Bentham's attacks on the common law as fictitious are notorious. First, the common law is full of technical legal fictions, which Bentham denounces as judicial subterfuges designed to reform the law by usurping proper authority from the

---

33. Bentham, "Essay on Language," 329. Bentham also says: "A word is a *sign of thought* . " in his "Essay on Logic," in *Works*, Vol. 8: 213–293 at 242. John Wisdom retorts: "But words are not signs of thought in the sense that they mean thoughts nor in the sense that they always refer to thoughts." *Interpretation and Analysis* 37–38.

34. As Postema says: "Language directly signifies our thoughts and ideas; thus, it does not (cannot) mirror accurately the actual structure of the external world." See his "Facts, Fiction, and Law," 54.

35. Postema, "Facts, Fiction, and Law," 47.

36. Bentham, *Of Laws in General* [hereafter OLG], Ed. H.L.A. Hart (University of London: Athlone Press, 1970) 16 and 193.

legislature.[37] Second, common law legal reasoning rests upon the fiction that judges "find" the law in custom, whereas in truth, says Bentham, they create new law, again usurping legislative authority.[38] Third, common law justifies itself by claiming that it rests upon the consent of the people, who are presumed to know their own customs; but, says Bentham, this confuses popular custom (*in pays*) with judicial custom (*in foro*): common law is primarily judicial custom, known only to lawyers and judges.[39] These fictions are condemned by Bentham as deliberate lies promulgated by lawyers to promote their own sinister interests; that is, he claims that the common law is a racket that benefits lawyers, who thus have no interest in dispelling these lucrative fictions.[40]

According to Bentham, all of these deliberate deceptions rest upon a deeper metaphysical fiction, and until that fiction is dissolved, the liars cannot be unmasked. Unlike the fictions of common law, metaphysical fictions are an inescapable part of human language and thought. "Fiction in the logical sense, has been the coin of necessity...that of the priest and the lawyer of mischievous immorality in the shape of mischievous ambition..."[41] Making reference to fictitious entities, says Bentham, is "necessary and indispensable" which is why he calls a metaphysical fiction a "blameless falsehood..."[42] The deeper metaphysical fiction is that the common law as a whole is a fictitious entity: "the Common Law is a thing merely imaginary..." (*Comment* 119). As with any fictitious entity, we can make sense of it only by relating it to real entities. What is the real entity that common law must be resolved into? Bentham says that although common law is temporally prior to statute law, statute law is logically prior to common law: we can understand common law only as a defective form of statute law.[43] We explain the common law "by shewing

---

37. "A fiction of law may be defined—a willful falsehood, having for its object the stealing of legislative power..." Bentham, *A Fragment of Government* (Hereafter *Fragment*), Eds. J.H. Burns and H.L.A. Hart (Oxford: Clarendon Press, 2008) 509.

38. "I hope it is by this time pretty apparent, that what is called the Unwritten Law is made not by the people but by Judges..." Bentham, *Comment* 223.

39. "They [the people] are supposed to know the Common Law: it is their own Custom; they make it of themselves. Such is the gibberish with which Lawyers blush not to insult the public." Bentham, *Comment* 320.

40. Of legal fiction: "It has never been employed but to a bad purpose." Bentham, "Constitutional Code," in *Works*. Vol. 9: 77. And: "the Law in its present confused state, is a monopoly which is established in their favour, and which for that reason they have no wish to break." Bentham, *Comment* 320.

41. Bentham, "Ontology," 199.

42. See Bentham, "Essay on Language," 327–328.

43. "In order of existence therefore the Common Law stands first: but in due order of intellection and instruction, in the order in which it can best be understood and easiest explained now that we have the other, it as certainly comes last." Bentham, *Comment* 119.

in what respect it approaches to the nature of the whole together and of the several articles of the Statute Law" (*Comment* 119). Why is statute law the real entity while common law is fictitious? Because, according to Bentham, a statute is the essential form of all law: "A law may be defined as an assemblage of signs declarative of a volition conceived or adopted by the sovereign in a state" (OLG, 1). This definition applies directly only to statute, which is why Bentham says: "Common law is but the shadow of the Statute Law" (*Comment* 119). Law is essentially a command (or permission) of the sovereign: "The Statute Law is composed of commands. The Common Law, of quasi-commands" (*Fragment* 430). Shadows reveal real objects only when we recognize that they are logically parasitic on physical bodies; common law reveals real law only when we recognize the rules of common law as parasitic on the commands of statutory law. Just as a tacit expression of will makes sense only by reference to a verbal expression of will, so the tacit commands of the common law make sense only by reference to the verbal commands of statute (*Fragment* 429–430). Metaphysical fictions, says Bentham, are allegories that must be decoded or riddles that must be solved if we are to "obtain a clear perception of the real state of things" (OLG 251).

In several places, Bentham distinguishes two main strategies for resolving fictitious entities into real entities. The first strategy is the etymological investigation of the concrete image or "archetype" that the word originally elicited in the mind of its users. According to Bentham, abstract words are all originally rooted in concrete pictures; over time, however, we have lost the original pictures conjured by our abstract language. As Bentham says: "*Archetypation*...consists in indicating the *material image*, of which the word, taken in its primeval sense, contains the expression" (*Chrestomathia* 272). If we are to understand the true meaning of our own abstract terms for fictitious entities, then we must bring back into focus the archetypal images of the real entities at the root of abstract words.[44] As Bentham puts it, "As in the case of all words, which have an immaterial, as well as a material, the root of the *immaterial* will be found in the *material* import..."(*Chrestomathia* 271). To use Nietzsche's famous metaphor for the same etymological analysis, abstract words are like coins

[44] "Archeypation, i.e. the origin of the psychological, in some physical idea, is often, in a manner, lost;—its physical marks, being more or less obliterated by the frequency of its use on psychological ground. . . " Bentham, "Essay on Logic," 246. Abstract words, he says, must be expounded "in terms calculated to raise *images* either of *substances* perceived, or of *emotions*; sources, one or other of which every idea must be drawn from, to be a clear one." Bentham, *Fragment* 495.

whose original images have been worn away by usage. Abstract words are allegories whose meaning is "dis-covered" by revealing the concrete physical picture at the root of the word. Bentham calls this method of uncovering the original real entity hidden within terms for fictitious entities a "genealogy" because he says it reveals the "genesis of the fictitious entity" (*Chrestomathia* 271). One example Bentham uses of this method of "archetypation" is with the word "spirit": the name of a fictitious entity whose concrete and archetypal meaning is "breath."[45] Once we reveal "breath" to be the real entity at the root of the word spirit, then we have dispelled the power of the word "spirit" to delude us.

The second main strategy for resolving fictitious entities into real ones is conceptual rather than lexical. In the procedure of what Bentham calls "paraphrasis," we take a proposition containing the name of a fictitious entity and translate that proposition into another proposition containing the name of a real entity.[46] Paraphrasis embodies Bentham's pioneering claim that the meaning of a word can be captured only in a proposition.[47] Paraphrasis is the name of a procedure whereby abstract and fictitious ideas are reduced to concrete and real ones. Thus, Bentham says that "the words *duties* and *rights* are here spoken of as names of fictitious entities." So how does the procedure of paraphrasis resolve them into real ones? First, for propositions asserting rights, Bentham substitutes propositions imposing duties. According to Bentham, the meaning of rights is exhausted by the statements of the duties those rights impose upon others. Having thus translated the language of rights into the language of duties, Bentham translates the language of duties into the language of pleasure and pain. One can be said to have a duty just insofar as one is liable to a painful sanction for the breach of that duty. Thus, the fictitious entities of rights and duties are translated into propositions about the real entities of pleasure and pain. Thus, the procedure of paraphrasis, which began with amorphous and vague abstractions, resolves the rhetoric of rights into a pointed inquiry about the real foundation of duty: "whether, supposing no

45. "In speaking of any *pneumatic* (or say *immaterial* or *spiritual*) object, no name has ever been employed, that had not first been employed as the name of some material (or say *corporeal*) one." Bentham, *Chrestomathia* 259.

46. "The *paraphrasis* consists in taking the word that requires to be expounded—viz. the name of a fictitious entity—and, after making it up into a *phrase*, applying to it another phrase, which, being of the same import, shall have for its principal and characteristic word the name of the corresponding *real* entity." Bentham, *Chrestomathia* 272.

47. Bentham's focus on propositions as the basic unit of meaning is called the basis of his main innovations as a philosopher by Hart (*Essays on Bentham*, 10) and then by Ross Harrison in *Bentham*, 64–66.

such sensations as *pleasure* or *pain, duties* would not be altogether without *force*, and *rights* altogether without *value*?" (*Chrestomathia* 272n).

Bentham nicely contrasts the conceptual focus of paraphrasis with the lexical focus of archetypation: "in the case of the name of a fictitious entity, a distinction requires to be made between the *root* of the idea, and the *root* of the *word* by which it is designated." With the example of "obligation," Bentham argues that paraphrasis leads us to the root of the idea, which is pleasure and pain, while archetypation leads us to the root of the word, which is the image of a person being tied up or bound.[48] In both cases, says Bentham, the object is to translate expressions containing the names of fictitious entities into expressions that conjure vivid images of real entities. We aim to find "terms calculated to raise *images* either of *substantives* perceived, or of *emotions*; sources, one or other of which every idea must be drawn from, to be a clear one."[49] Thus, he reduces the term "obligation" to an image of a substantive perceived (a man tied up) and to a vivid emotion (pleasure or pain). Of course, the procedure of paraphrasis is illuminating only to the degree that one is persuaded that the language of rights can be translated, without loss, into the language of the sensations of pleasure and pain. In short, Bentham's strategies for resolving what he calls fictitious entities into real ones rests upon his metaphysics; yet, as we have seen, his metaphysics is incoherent because Bentham cannot decide whether the foundation of real entities is in individual things, physical bodies, or mental sensations.

Returning to Bentham's analysis of common law as a fictitious entity, we can see in his early *Comment* the rudiments of Bentham's twofold analysis. First, Bentham focuses on the word "law" and considers the original "archetype" of that word, that is, the image first formed in the mind by the word "law." Bentham argues that law "had for its archetype some sensible symbol of the Legislator's will" (*Comment* 118–119). But this exercise in archetypation has no basis in etymology, unlike Bentham's analysis of "spirit" or "obligation." Moreover, Bentham argues that common law came before statute law, so the original use of the expression "common law" cannot have had the archetype for law: "Tis the Statute Law then that first suggested the idea we have (when we have *any*) belonging to the word *Law*" (*Comment* 119). So the name of the fictitious entity common *law* remains a mystery: the archetype for law is the archetype for statute

---

48. Bentham, *Chrestomathia* 272n. Curiously, for a gifted linguist, Bentham elsewhere offers a totally different etymology of the word "obligation": he says that "the archetypal image, is that of a man lying down with a heavy body pressing upon him." See "Essay on Logic," 247.
49. Bentham, *Fragment* 495.

law. If Bentham had argued that common law arose subsequently to statute law, then archetypation would have revealed the real entity (sovereign command) at the root of the fictitious entity of common law. But Bentham insists that "in order of existence therefore the Common Law stands first" (*Comment* 119). Thus, as a "genealogy" of the word law, Bentham's archetypation fails to account for the use of the expression "common law." Indeed, when Bentham attempts to reconstruct the origins of common law, he arrives at custom: "before any Laws, any commands destined for universal and durable obedience were issued, States being notwithstanding formed, the people of them were governed, as it were from hand to mouth by sets of that sort of transient and particular rules of which in great part is composed what is stiled the Common Law" (*Comment* 119). But if custom ruled before the commands of law, then why was that rule of custom known as common law? We might note that if Bentham had found a different archetype for law (such as the image of a convention) then he would have seen that there was law before statute law. Second, as for paraphrasis, he doesn't use this word in the *Comment* but he uses paraphrasis to expound the idea of law into propositions about commands, which are enforced by sanctions, which refer to the distribution of punishments, which are kinds of pain (*Comment* 119). So archetypation leads us to law as command while paraphrasis leads us all the way back to pain.

Bentham argues further that statute law is real in a way in which common law is not because statute law is composed of real, visible, and individual statutes: "The Statute Law is a body composed of members we are acquainted with.... We see, we hear, we touch: in short, we handle them. . .what is the *Common Law*? What, but an assemblage of fictitious regulations feigned after the images of these real ones that compose the Statute Law?" (*Comment* 119–120). So the Statute Law is itself another fiction in the sense that statute law is an abstract name that means nothing more than an assemblage of real individual statutes. The reduction of statute law to individual statutes is the typical Benthamite reduction of the abstract fiction into real material parts. Yet, this reduction was only provisional because Bentham later realized that individual laws did not correspond to individual statutes: a law turns out to be an abstract idea that cannot be reduced to a material statute. "The idea of a law (in its primary sense) is the idea of an object which may be purely intellectual existing nowhere but in the mind of him who speaks of it: the idea of a statute is constantly the idea of a material object, copies of which may be had anywhere at the booksellers.... Laws in short are the elements of which statutes are composed, and into which in order to be understood they must be resolved" (OLG, 12). The conceptual individuation of laws does not lead to individual statutes.

Bentham frequently applied his metaphysics of individuation to law. Indeed, he claims that no domain of knowledge requires the method of individuation more than law.[50] But it is important to note that individuation can yield both physical wholes and logical wholes. Using the example of the word "plant," Bentham argues that with respect to physical wholes, "plant" is a fictitious entity, a mere label to sort real physical organisms: "Nor let it be said, that, because it contains real entities, the aggregate, called a species, a genus, a class, is itself a real entity." With respect to mind-independent reality, terms for aggregates are fictitious entities, in the sense that there is no physical entity corresponding to "plant"; outside of the mind, there are only individual plants. But in addition to physical wholes, such as individual plants, there are also logical wholes, such as "plant," that exist within the mind, but are no less real than physical wholes. So the same word "plant," which is a fictitious entity in relation to physical plants, becomes a real entity in relation to the mind: "a *general idea*,—an entity, which though not *corporeal*, is not less *real* than that which is produced in it by the sight or touch of an individual plant."[51] Indeed, Bentham even says that we have more evidence of the reality of the general idea "plant" than we have evidence of the reality of individual plants.[52] In short, we can individuate plant into physical plants and we can individuate the general idea of plant into a logical whole, by specifying the unique and "distinguishable mental sensations" produced by the idea of "plant." Bentham similarly begins by individuating law into the physical wholes of visible statutes, but later he favors individuating law into the logical whole of a "complete law." In these two modes of individuation we see the contrary pulls of Bentham's metaphysics: reducing law to a set of physical wholes reflects his materialism, while reducing law to a set of logical wholes reflects his phenomenalism. The fact that he argues that logical wholes can be just as real as physical wholes, proves that his ideal of a complete law indeed rests upon his ontology of real and fictitious entities.[53]

---

50. "The field of *law* is the field in which the demand for this mode of individuation, for this mode of exposition, is most copious and most urgent. . . " ("Essay on Logic," 243).

51. *Chrestomathia* 265n.

52. "Of the evidence of the existence of the general idea, the probative force is even nearer, and more promptly and surely satisfactory, than that of the existence of any individual plant. . . " *Chrestomathia* 265n.

53. According to Postema, Bentham's ideal of a complete law "is not an ontological notion at all." *Bentham and the Common Law Tradition* 300.

Custom as Fiction

Although Bentham often says that "the customary [i.e. common] law is a fiction" (OLG 193), to my knowledge, he never explicitly asserts that custom itself is a fictitious entity. Curiously, Bentham relentlessly individuates "custom" and "habit" into physical wholes and never contemplates custom or habit as a logical whole. Bentham describes custom sometimes as an aggregate of habits and at other times as an aggregate of acts, whereas he always defines habits as an aggregate of acts. His nominalism requires him to define all such class concepts as fictitious. Although habits are predicated of individuals, customs are properly predicated only of communities. Yet, Bentham asserts that "the community is a fictitious *body*, composed of individual persons."[54] So custom is a fictitious quality of a fictitious body. Another way to define custom is to say that it is a relation, based on convention, among the habits of individual persons. But Bentham argues that all relations are fictitious entities,[55] meaning that there is no real basis for custom as a conventional relation among the habits of individuals. But if custom were merely an assemblage of the habits of individuals, then there would be no distinction between similar but private habits and truly common social customs. Often, as we shall see, Bentham reduces custom to habit, since habits belong to individual persons; but Bentham also frequently tells us that "habit is a fictitious entity,"[56] since a habit is composed of discrete acts. Thus, for Bentham, habits are class concepts as well as invisible, whereas human acts are both individual and visible, and thus real (*Principles* 78n).

Bentham never attempts an etymological investigation of "custom" or "habit" as a way of uncovering the original, material archetype of those words, as do many philosophers of custom. Instead, Bentham's nominalism leads him to reduce custom to habit and habit to individual act; at the same time, Bentham's phenomenalism will lead him to reduce custom to legal sanction and ultimately to pain. What is lost in these reductions is the irreducible social dimension of custom: the informal conventions of custom and the role of informal sanctions in custom. If we were to aggregate the actions and habits of individual persons ad seriatim, we would never

---

54. Bentham, *An Introduction to the Principles of Moral and Legislation* [hereafter *Principles*] Eds. J.H. Burns and H.L.A. Hart (University of London: Athlone Press, 1970) 12.

55. Bentham, "Ontology," 203.

56. Bentham *Deontology*, Ed. Amnon Goldworth (Oxford: Clarendon Press, 1983) 349. See also *Principles* 78n and 119n.

reach a custom, since we could not distinguish the mere coincidence of private habits from true social customs.

Similarly, in his reduction of habit to individual acts, Bentham obscures the dispositional nature of habits. According to Bentham: "A *habit* is but an assemblage of *acts*. . . " (*Fragment* 429n). Bentham's nominalism leads him to think of the term "habit" as a class concept—just as "automobile" is but a convenient label for an assemblage of vehicles, so "habit" is just a convenient label for an assemblage of acts. But a closer analogy to the relation of habits to acts would be that of syntax to words. Is a sentence just an assemblage of words? Or does "sentence" refer, not simply to an assemblage of words, but equally to the syntax that unites them? Here Bentham's phenomenalism reinforces his nominalism: we can see "acts" and "words" but not habits or syntax, which must be inferred. As a linguist, Bentham recognizes that the meaning of any particular word cannot be grasped apart from a complete sentence. But as a social theorist, Bentham does not see that a particular act cannot be understood apart from the personal habit or social custom that gives it meaning. Is a necklace "an assemblage of pearls" simply because we don't see the string that unites them? Are the pearls real while the string a mere fiction? Yes, according to Bentham, the acts are real but the habit fictitious: "A habit, it should seem, can hardly in strictness be termed an aggregate of acts: acts being a sort of real archetypal entities, and habits a kind of fictitious entities or imaginary beings, supposed to be constituted by, or to result as it were out of, the former" (*Principles* 78n). In Bentham's ontology, there are only individual acts and nothing real holding them together: "Strictly speaking, habit, being but a fictitious entity, and not really any thing distinct from the acts or perceptions by which it is said to be formed, cannot be the cause of any thing" (*Principles* 119n). So, words are real, but syntax fictitious; pearls are real, but strings fictitious.[57] We can now see why custom is equally fictitious: "A custom is an assemblage of acts. . . " (*Comment* 185). But customs, not acts, are the true unit of meaning in social life.

Bentham's most sustained analysis of custom is from his commentary on Blackstone. Here Bentham argues that custom is merely a collective habit: "Custom. . . is referred either to a single person or to a multitude" (*Comment* 181). Thus, Bentham claims that the term "custom" is used univocally of both individuals and communities. He demonstrates this with the example: "It is my custom to go in term time to Westminster Hall"

---

[57]. Bentham indeed does define language as an assemblage of words: "that assemblage of conventional signs which taken collectively are called *language*" (OLG 82).

which is merely multiplied to become "It is the custom of Barristers to go in term time to Westminster Hall" (*Comment* 181). Bentham is certainly right that the word custom is commonly used as a synonym for habit, but that fact is perfectly compatible with there being a fundamental conceptual difference between custom and habit. Habits are psychological dispositions of individual persons; customs are social conventions rooted in individual habits. Habits can be purely idiosyncratic but customs are always common to a community.[58] I might have a habit of taking exercise by going to Westminster Hall, but barristers go to Westminster Hall in term time because they know that their colleagues will also go there and they know that their colleagues know that they know to go to Westminster Hall, etc. The common knowledge shared by all barristers is the basis of a custom, but not of many individual habits. The reality of this common knowledge is lost if we reduce social customs to individual habits on the grounds that common knowledge is not tangible or visible. We don't see social conventions; all we see is the coincidence of individual behavior. But the custom of barristers going in term time to Westminster is not merely a coincidence of individual habits. We cannot multiply habits in order to get custom.

Bentham's tendency to reduce custom to habit is also manifest in his view that customs describe conduct in the past tense: custom refers to what I have done, not what I shall do. He says that it would be preposterous to say "it is my custom that I shall go in term time to Westminster" (*Comment* 181). Elsewhere, Bentham says that a habit tells us what was done in the past while a disposition tells us what we shall do in the future (*Fragment* 488). Bentham is right in claiming that if we think of customs merely as group habits, then they must be rooted in the past. Continuing to speak of grammatical tense, Bentham goes on to say that when customs become enforced by lawwe speak of them in the future tense. That is, regarding mere customs, we say: "It has been the custom of the Judges to go in term time to Westminster Hall": but once those customs become enforced by law, we say: "It is the custom that the Judges *shall* go to Westminster Hall in term time" (*Comment* 182). At this early date, Bentham had not yet worked out his sophisticated deontological grammar and logic, but still these claims about grammatical tense are wholly unconvincing. The most natural "tense" for habits or customs is the imperfect tense, which characterizes actions that began in the past but continue into the present. Moreover, legal mandates can be framed in the present tense as easily as

[58] Postema criticizes Bentham for ignoring the difference here between social customs and idiosyncratic habits in his *Bentham and the Common Law Tradition* 222.

in the future: "If a judge does not go to Westminster Hall in term time, he is subject to the following sanctions. . . " It is clear why Bentham looks to grammatical tense to distinguish informal custom from legal custom: it provides an empirical procedure for verifying the existence of custom, since we look to past behavior to establish habits or custom and we look to future behavior to test the predictions of law. Here, as elsewhere, Bentham seems unduly influenced by Blackstone, who also claimed that customs must exist "from time beyond memory." Yet, once we understand that customs often serve as coordinating conventions, we see that they do not necessarily rest upon the past: what matters is the pattern of expectations now, not the past. The contemporary philosophical analysis of dispositions, habitual or customary, is not in terms of grammatical tense at all but in terms of grammatical mood. Dispositions are now said to characterize actions in the subjunctive mood: they tell us what we would do, were certain conditions present. Dispositions are counterfactual conditionals. But, for Bentham, to explain habits in terms of counterfactual conditionals would merely be to substitute one fiction for another, even more mysterious fiction.

Custom and Obligation

Bentham associates the future tense with obligation: obligations, he says, apply only to prospective or future conduct. An obligation applied de novo to past conduct would violate the fundamental precepts of justice against ex post facto laws and retroactive punishment. So when Bentham makes his fundamental distinction between what he calls "spontaneous" and "legalized" customs, he marks this distinction grammatically. He says that "spontaneous" customs refer to the past because they involve no obligations while "legalized" customs involve obligation and so therefore refer to the future. Bentham's claim that spontaneous customs involve no obligation is deeply puzzling.[59] Speaking of legalized customs, Bentham asks, "And whence comes that obligation? What is it that constitutes it? What, but their being exposed to punishment in the case of their not observing it. . . " (*Comment* 182). Bentham says that "a custom *obligatory*" is identical to "a custom *legalized*" (*Comment* 183). Moreover, "*Custom* is not in itself any thing that can compel: *Law* is" (*Comment* 308). This view that customs become obligatory only when enforced by law contradicts

---

59. Postema criticizes Bentham here for not noting that all "social or group customs are to some extent prescriptive." See Postema, *Bentham and the Common Law* 222.

all human experience. Customs are everywhere enforced by moral, social, and religious sanctions. These sanctions are very effective, as evidenced by the fact that an adult man is much more likely, statistically, to commit murder than to wear women's clothes in public. Consequently, Bentham's definition here of obligation in terms of legal punishment alone is puzzling since even in the *Comment*, Bentham distinguishes legal from moral and religious sanctions (42, 82–83). He also frequently says that these three kinds of sanctions give rise to three kinds of duties (e.g., *Fragment* 496n). Bentham defines the moral sanction, not as the reproach of conscience, but as "reward or punishment at the hands of men, unliquidated by Law" (*Comment* 83). So Bentham elsewhere seems to acknowledge that spontaneous custom gives rise to genuine duties backed by informal punishment.

Bentham shows a curious desire to restrict the use of the word "obligation" to mean "legal obligation." In his discussion of the custom and law of bailment, Bentham acknowledges that even before common law took notice, carriers were by custom liable to make good any loss or damage of goods entrusted to them. "They were not obliged: they were not obliged, that is, by the political Sanction. *Determined* at the same time they were: by what? By considerations of what is called Natural justice enforced by the moral Sanction" (*Comment* 334). Once judges began to enforce this custom at law, says Bentham, "It was their custom before to do so: to observe this custom they now felt themselves *obliged*" (*Comment* 335). Here we find Bentham playing word games while he concedes that spontaneous custom gives rise to duties enforced by the moral sanction. Perhaps Bentham realizes that if he fully acknowledges that spontaneous custom generates moral obligations, then his critique of common law as retroactive "dog law" fails: usually judges at common law are merely enforcing what are already known to be moral obligations. Law merely provides a more certain sanction.

What is the moral authority of custom? Spontaneous custom would seem to be free of some of Bentham's famous critiques of common law. Bentham sharply attacked Blackstone's arguments that common law is publicly promulgated because it rests upon custom. Bentham argues that legalized customs (whether customs *in pays* or customs *in foro*) are made by judges and promulgated by judges to lawyers, since legalized customs are not promulgated to, let alone made by, the people (*Comment* 191). Hence, the people cannot be expected to know which of their customs will be enforced by law, leading to Bentham's conclusions that common law is unjustly retroactive. But Bentham concedes that the people can be assumed to know spontaneous custom: "How is it known? Meaning by the people? Why, they know it by the supposition; they even practice it, it is their custom" (*Comment* 192). Hence, the informal enforcement of spontaneous custom cannot be unjustly retroactive: custom is promulgated in the informal practices of the people and known by them. Spontaneous custom thus has for Bentham an undeniable moral superiority over legalized custom.

Blackstone also defends the moral authority of spontaneous custom on the grounds that not only is custom known to the people, but the people consent to their customs. Custom, in this view, has a kind of democratic legitimacy. Blackstone quotes the ancient Roman jurist Julian who argues that the people consent to their customs by practicing them just as they consent to proposed laws by voting for them: "For where is the difference, whether the people declare their assent to a law by suffrage, or by a uniform course of acting accordingly?" Blackstone draws this conclusion from Julian about the common law: "it is one of the characteristic marks of English liberty, that our common law depends upon custom; which carries this internal evidence of freedom along with it, that it probably was introduced by the voluntary consent of the people."[60] Bentham's response to this assertion reveals his tendency to focus on legalized custom rather than on spontaneous custom: "The fallacy lies in the abusive application of the term 'assent': in the giving to a uniform course of action according to a Law, after that Law is passed, and punishment threatened for the breach of it, that same name 'assent,' as is given to an express declaration of the concurrence of the party's will with the Law before its passing" (*Comment* 221). Thus, whereas Blackstone takes Julian to be comparing voting to spontaneous custom, Bentham takes Julian to be comparing voting for a law to conforming to that law when passed. Clearly, Blackstone is right about Julian, who is speaking explicitly of spontaneous custom (*mos* and *consuetudo*).[61] Unfortunately, because of Bentham's misreading we are denied his answer to Julian's question: do people consent to their customs?

Bentham approaches the issue of consent to custom elsewhere by arguing that if customs are obligatory, then we cannot be said to consent to them. He quotes Blackstone: "Customs, though established by consent, must be when established, compulsory: and not left to the option of every man, whether he will use them or no." Bentham responds by once again confusing legal obligation with all obligations: "This notion of legal obligation starting up in the way of equivocal generation without a productive

---

60. Blackstone, *Commentaries on the Laws of England,* Introduction, Sec. 3.
61. See Julian in *Digest* I, 3.32.

cause is somewhat whimsical" (*Comment* 248). Bentham cannot here imagine how custom might become obligatory without being enforced by law.[62] Bentham then attacks the claim that custom could be both compulsory and consensual: "are consent and compulsion then the same? Is it the same to consent to do a thing, and to be compelled to do it?" (*Comment* 249). How can we consent to customs that are obligatory? If Bentham had thought of customs, not merely as constraints but also as enabling conventions, he would have seen that we have good reasons to consent to be bound by custom. We recognize that we need coordination in certain domains of life (who pays for the marriage?), we recognize that the expectations of the community have settled upon a particular solution to this coordination problem (the bride's family), and hence, we consent to be bound by that convention.

Bentham even argues that if all customs are obligatory, then it follows that there are no spontaneous customs: "Purely spontaneous there must be none. They must all be [legally] compulsory" (*Comment* 249). What does Bentham mean by "spontaneous" custom? He contrasts "spontaneous" with "legal" custom: spontaneous customs receive no recognition by law while legal custom is enforced by law. But Bentham also means by this contrast, that spontaneous customs are always purely optional while legal customs alone are obligatory: "Custom in its ordinary and popular signification, in which the acts of which it denotes the assemblage are all spontaneous, at least for anything that results from Law. . . " (*Comment* 182). Bentham's use of the word "spontaneous" here is ambiguous: first, custom is spontaneous if it arises willy-nilly as a by-product of human actions, rather than being imposed by law; second, custom could also be spontaneous if it were always regarded as purely optional by each individual person. Bentham seems to assume that the first sense implies the second, which, as we see with the example of paying for weddings, it does not. Moreover, if a course of conduct were purely optional for each person, that very fact would show that there is no applicable custom. Customs, as conventions, cannot coordinate expectations and behavior if they leave the relevant conduct purely to spontaneous choice. Where choices are purely spontaneous and optional, custom, like law, must be silent. Bentham argues further that no custom that favors one party over the other could be maintained except by legal compulsion: "A custom which is active on the side of one party at whose expense it is maintained can seldom be

62. Bentham goes on to refer to "the way in which an act or a custom originally spontaneous may be provisionally legalized, and thereby become compulsory. . . "

supposed to be spontaneous. . . The sense of moral obligation in such a case rarely has place: or though it should have place, would be too weak to overcome the joint influence of indolence and interest" (*Comment* 234). But, as the customs that the bride's family pays for the wedding and that a wife adopts her husband's name prove, customs that substantially burden one party over another can be quite stable without any support from legal compulsion.

Still, the fact that people often have good reasons to conform to the constraints of custom does not mean that people always ought to consent to their customs. Some customs enforce racial, class, and gender hierarchies. Subordinate groups might have good reasons to conform to these customs, but no good reasons to consent to them. Is the sheer fact that we practice a custom strong evidence that we consent to it? As we saw above, in his discussion of the Hindu custom of sati, Bentham does not assume that a widow's conformity to this custom proves her consent. He would permit her to immolate herself on her dead husband's pyre only if she does so voluntarily: "but such permission should not be granted till after she had undergone an examination and the fact of her consent were indubitably ascertained."[63] So Bentham at least implicitly rejects Julian's argument that people express their consent as much by their practices as by their votes.

Custom as the Unity of Habit and Convention

Gerald Postema takes Bentham of the *Comment* to task for reducing customs to habits, for reducing both customs and habits to assemblages of past acts, and for neglecting the prescriptive dimension of custom: "if Bentham had left the matter here we would have to conclude that his account of custom is extremely crude." But, says Postema, if we look at other writings of Bentham, we can reconstruct from these scattered pieces a much more adequate theory of custom "nearly as sophisticated as Hume's."[64] Postema is certainly right that we can indeed locate elements of Bentham's thought with which to construct a more sophisticated theory of custom. However, as I briefly explore Postema's reconstruction of Bentham's theory, I will argue that Bentham does not escape the limitations of his reductionism as much as Postema suggests, and that with respect to the conventional dimension of custom, Bentham falls far short of Hume.

---

63. Bentham, "Place and Time," 174.

64. Postema, *Bentham and the Common Law Tradition* 222–223.

What is the relation of custom to its own rationale? Postema rightly points out that Bentham's frequent descriptions of custom as mere assemblages of past acts is not the whole story, since Bentham also, following Blackstone, discusses the relationship of customs to maxims (that is, propositional rules): "A custom is an assemblage of acts. . . What then is a maxim? Is this too an assemblage of acts? Nothing like it. What then is it? A species of discourse, a proposition. . . " (*Comment* 185). The context is common law reasoning in which judges work with two very different aspects of cases: the pattern of facts (what Bentham calls the "custom") and the rule said to capture the unity of those facts. "'Tis the course of action itself that is the custom: and the proposition announcing it that is the maxim" (*Comment* 304). Given Bentham's metaphysics, we can see why he thinks that the course of action is empirically objective even if rules are subjective and inferential.[65] Bentham's ontology itself creates a chasm between the custom and the rule, but Bentham has further reasons for wanting to drive a wedge between the pattern of conduct that constitutes the custom and the verbal rationale of that conduct formulated in a rule. Bentham devotes several pages of the *Comment* to arguing that the rules or maxims that formally "announce" a custom are often very misleading and inaccurate guides to the actual customs. According to Bentham, the maxim "the King can do no wrong" is a very inaccurate interpretation of the set of customs related to sovereign immunity (*Comment* 185–188). Bentham does not argue that all maxims are purely arbitrary, but he does argue that any pattern of conduct will likely admit of more than one maxim. Just as philosophers of science often say that scientific theories are under-determined by the data they purport to explain, so Bentham argues that legal rules are under-determined by the customs they purportedly "announce."

But how is this critique of common law reasoning relevant to the theory of custom itself? Postema concedes that Bentham's discussion of the relation of custom to rules is within the context of common law, but he says that Bentham's "account can easily be generalized to cover custom *in pays* as well."[66] Postema does not attempt to generalize to spontaneous custom, but we might pause to consider how it might work, taking the example of some of the customs defining courtesy.[67] If we observe a pattern of

65. "Unlike the concrete, publicly accessible acts comprising the custom, rules of the custom are arrived at by inference, not by observation." Postema, *Bentham and the Common Law Tradition* 225.
66. Postema, *Bentham and the Common Law Tradition* 225.
67. See Ronald Dworkin's discussion of how to interpret "courtesy" in *Law's Empire* (Cambridge: Harvard University Press, 1986) 47–52. My examples differ from Dworkin's.

conduct, say, for instance, a man opening a door for a woman, what rule or rules might we formulate to capture that pattern? There are many obvious possibilities, ranging from, "one should always assist others who may benefit from such assistance," to, "adult men should offer their strength to women and children." But, as observers of these customs of courtesy, we are in a fundamentally different position from observers of patterns of the behavior of inanimate objects. In the case of a scientist attempting to formulate a generalization to capture an observed regularity, there really is a chasm between the empirically objective data and the subjective interpretation of that data by an observer. But in the case of custom, the maxim or rule is already implicit in the "assemblage of acts" that constitute the custom: everyone who practices courtesy acts partly from a maxim defining the point of that practice. He might not verbally rehearse that maxim while he opens a door, but if asked why he habitually opens doors for other people, he might formulate a rule, ranging from "women and children need assistance" to "I assist everyone who needs help." We could test the adequacy of his formulated maxim to see how well it fits with his other actions; he might well acknowledge a gap between his implicit maxim and his formulated maxim. However, this only serves to illustrate that the observer of customs, unlike the observer of inanimate objects, is likely to practice an analogous custom, and so will have his own maxim. Indeed, without possessing an analogous maxim, it is hard to see how an observer could even identify the relevant assemblage of acts that partly constitute the custom. In short, even though in common law, the factual patterns of customs and the judicial maxims are distinct, in the lived reality of custom, rules are inseparable from the assemblage of acts they describe. If I have a disposition to be courteous, then, in the specified circumstances, I will tend to act in accordance with my personal interpretation of what courtesy means. I may be disposed to help women and children in a wide range of situations or I may be disposed to help anyone who needs assistance in a narrower range of situations. Customs are not "an assemblage of acts" plus "a propositional rule";[68] rather, customs are a course of conduct unified and animated by at least implicit rules. In customs, we are disposed to think and to feel just as much as we are disposed to act. Postema is right that we need to complement Bentham's reduction of custom to an assemblage of acts with his account of rules and maxims. But Bentham's description of

---

68. Postema summarizes Bentham's reconstructed and more "sophisticated" theory of custom as a pattern of acts "plus" a propositional rule. *Bentham and the Common Law Tradition* 225.

how acts relate to rules in custom remains, in Postema's words, "extremely crude."

We saw above that Bentham very frequently in the *Comment* denies that customs create obligations unless and until they are enforced by law. We also saw, however, that in his discussion of the custom of bailment, Bentham acknowledged that even before the common law took notice of bailment, owners expected carriers to be answerable for damage or loss to their goods. Bentham conceded that these expectations of owners create moral obligations for carriers, what he calls duties of natural justice.[69] So we can see that Bentham acknowledges the prescriptive force of custom where it gives rise to legitimate expectations. This framework of mutual expectations creates a very different picture of Bentham's theory: "Custom, for Bentham, we can now see, is not merely a matter of uniformity of 'exterior' actions, a matter of mere coincidence of habits of people. Rather, it is essentially *interactional*." Postema concedes: "This interactional, or interdependent, character of custom is not always clearly brought out by Bentham...."[70] Indeed, as we have seen, Bentham's ontology of fictitious entities makes it very difficult for him to acknowledge the real generality of habits and custom, which Bentham often dissolves into mere aggregates of acts. Even Bentham's discussion of mutual expectations falls well short of the requirements of the modern theory of conventions as resting on "common knowledge." In his discussion of the customs of bailment, Bentham never suggests that owners expect carriers to know that owners expect them to indemnify their goods. In short, Bentham's account of expectations is additive: each individual's expectations are added to those of the other relevant parties. But mutual expectations are much more deeply interdependent than Bentham suggests: I form my expectations in light of what I expect you to know of what I expect.

In his discussion of Bentham's theory of sovereignty, Postema also contrasts a crude "mechanical" with a more sophisticated "interactional" account of habit and custom. In the mechanical model, sovereign authority rests merely upon a habit or disposition of each person, individually, to obey regardless of what others are disposed to do. In the interactional model, an individual's disposition to obey will depend in part upon what he believes his fellow citizens are disposed to do. In this model, I am more likely to obey if I believe you will obey. In the mechanical model, each

---

69. According to Postema: "Justice, for Bentham, is first of all a matter of respecting expectation utilities.... Justice consists in following the law where following maximizes respect for expectation utilities." Postema, *Bentham and the Common Law Tradition* 153.

70. Postema, *Bentham and the Common Law Tradition* 229.

person makes the decision to obey by his own lights and general obedience is the aggregate of those separate decisions; in the interactional model, the people come to a shared understanding of when to obey such that each person's decision depends upon his beliefs about what others are likely to do. There is textual evidence in Bentham for both interpretations. Postema, however, is persuasive that Bentham's account of sovereignty rests upon both habits and conventions.[71]

Yet, the concept of a convention is ambiguous: conventions can arise from deliberate stipulation, as with written constitutions; or from informal social practice, such as spontaneous customs; or from a mixture of both stipulation and practice. For example, both Esperanto and English serve as linguistic conventions, but we sometimes call English a "natural" language because the conventions of English were not deliberately stipulated, as with Esperanto, but arose from informal practice. Except when referring to the conventions of language, Bentham always uses the term "convention" to refer only to deliberately stipulated, legal conventions.[72] In short, for Bentham, all conventions, apart from linguistic conventions, are express conventions. Here the contrast with his philosophical master Hume could not be sharper. Hume offered several famous examples of how conventions can arise without any express agreement: "Two men, who pull the oars of a boat, do it by an agreement or convention, tho' they have never given promises to each other."[73] Hume used this example to illustrate how the customary conventions defining property rights could have emerged gradually over time.

In his discussion of the limits of sovereignty, Bentham first considers the deliberations of each person separately, who must weigh "the probable mischiefs of resistance" against "the probable mischiefs of submission." When the first mischiefs begin to outweigh the second, we have reached "the juncture for resistance." But Bentham sees here the need for a convention to mark this "juncture for resistance": "by what *sign* shall this juncture be known? By what *common* signal alike conspicuous and perceptible to all. . . " (*Fragment* 484). Bentham sees here that my disposition to obey the government will depend crucially on my knowing whether others will obey as well. But what signal shall the people communicate to each other that they have reached the "juncture for resistance"?

---

71. See Postema, *Bentham and the Common Law Tradition* 232–262.

72. "the connexion between a word and its import is altogether arbitrary, the result of tacit convention and long-continued usage." Bentham, "Essay on Logic," 238.

73. Hume, *Treatise of Human Nature*, Ed. L. A. Selby-Bigge, Rev. P. Nidditch (Oxford: Oxford University Press, 1978) 490.

Hume's rower's communicate to each other, by, say, matching stroke for stroke, but Bentham's subjects have no way to communicate the juncture for resistance to each other: "*Common* sign for such a purpose, I, for my part, know of none"; so each person is trapped in "his own internal persuasion of a balance of *utility* on the side of resistance." Without such a common sign, says, Bentham, sovereign authority is limited only by its own "express convention": "the authority of the supreme body cannot, *unless where limited by express convention*, be said to have any assignable, any certain bounds" (*Fragment* 484–485).

Later, Bentham argues that this "express convention" can serve as the "common signal" marking the "juncture for resistance": "By means of a convention then we are furnished with that common signal which, in other cases, we despaired of finding" (*Fragment* 489). This "express convention" or "common signal," says Bentham, is provision of a treaty or of a constitution limiting the powers of federated states. Oren Ben-Dor in his study of Bentham's constitutionalism sees a tension similar to Postema's. In searching for the "juncture for resistance," Bentham, says Ben-Dor, is torn between an "express convention to facilitate inter-subjective communication" and "each individual's subjective internal persuasion." In other words, resistance would arise from either a sheer coincidence of private individual judgments or from a true constitutional convention leading to "agreement." Ben-Dor believes that Bentham favors the option of consensus-building discussion and agreement.[74] Here we see the total absence in Bentham's account of any notion of an informal convention, since informal conventions arise precisely when agreements are not feasible. If ever there were a time when an agreement arising from an "express convention" is not feasible, it is the "juncture for resistance." In actual political history, those informal conventions usually involve large numbers of people spontaneously gathering in the streets to protest some governmental injustice. But Bentham can think of conventions only as formal, legal conventions.

Postema offers an example of Bentham's notion of a common signal in the context of customary practices discussed in the *Comment* (242): "He gives the example of the coordinated use of a common pasture on a manor, in which the Lord's putting out his cattle to graze on the commons was a signal to tenants to do so as well."[75] But even here, the convention did not

---

74. Ben-Dor, Oren. *Constitutional Limits and the Public Sphere* (Portland: Hart Publishing, 2000) 113–116. On the need for reaching "agreement," Ben-Dor cites Bentham's *Fragment* 491.
75. Postema, *Bentham and the Common Law Tradition* 246.

arise spontaneously but was imposed unilaterally by the lord of the manor. This convention is closer to Esperanto than to English: the lord stipulated the convention—the convention did not arise from accumulated practice. So Postema is right that sovereign authority for Bentham rests upon shared conventions, but these conventions are rooted in deliberate stipulation or agreement rather than in the tacit practices of custom.

Bentham often treated habits and conventions as alterative foundations of law rather than as the joint constituents of custom. In discussing the "disposition to obedience," Bentham says: "This disposition may have had for its cause either *habit* or *convention*: a convention announces the will of one moment, which the will of any other moment may revoke;—habit is the result of a system of conduct of which the commencement is lost in the abyss of time."[76] Here, by convention, Bentham clearly means an express declaration of a person or body; by habit, a long-standing course of conduct. What is largely missing in Bentham's account is a description of how conventions become habitualized and how habits become conventionalized: the essential nature of custom never comes into focus. In this respect, Bentham's theory of custom falls short of Hume's theory, as Postema concedes. Bentham's nominalism recognizes the reality only of individual entities; however, customs rest upon a real relation between individual habits and social conventions. Hence, customs escape the net of Bentham's logic.

---

[76]. Bentham, *Pannomial Fragments*, in *Works* Vol. 3: 211–230 at 219.

CHAPTER 4 | James C. Carter's Natural Law Theory of Custom

JAMES COOLIDGE CARTER (1827–1905) was perhaps the most renowned American legal advocate of the Gilded Age.[1] From his position as a leader of the American bar, Carter waged a 25-year campaign to defeat the efforts of David Dudley Field to codify the common law, especially the common law of New York State in the 1870s and 1880s. We only learn to value something when we fear losing it, and Carter did not come to appreciate the unique virtues of customary law until Field threatened to codify and replace it. In the course of defending his beloved customary law, Carter emerged as the leading American representative of the historical school of jurisprudence.[2] Indeed, the founder of the historical school, Friedrich

---

1. For Carter's legal career, his jurisprudence, and his politics, see Lewis A. Grossman, "James Coolidge Carter and Mugwamp Jurisprudence" in *Law and History Review* 20 (3) Fall 2002: 577–629. Available at SSRN: http://ssrn.com/abstract=1098262. And Grossman: "Langdell Upside-Down: James Coolidge Carter and the Anticlassical Jurisprudence of Anti-Codification." *Yale Journal of Law & the Humanities*, Vol. 19, 149, 2007; American University, WCL Research Paper No. 08-36. Available at SSRN: http://ssrn.com/abstract=897786 And Grossman, " 'The Benefits and Evils of Competition': James Coolidge Carter's Supreme Court Advocacy," in *Festschrift in Honor of Morton J. Horwitz*, Ed. Alfred Brophy and Daniel Hamilton (Cambridge: Harvard University Press, 2008).

2. As Grossman says, "Carter himself was almost completely unversed in legal theory before he joined the codification battle in the early 1880s. By his own admission, he familiarized himself with the jurisprudential literature and developed his own legal ideas about the origin and nature of law for the specific purpose of resisting codification." See Lewis A. Grossman, "From Savigny through Sir Henry Maine": Roscoe Pound's Flawed Portrait of James Coolidge Carter's Historical Jurisprudence (3). American University, WCL Research Paper No. 2009-21. Available at SSRN: http://ssrn.com/abstract=1407623 As the debate over the codification of the common law faded, so did scholarly interest in Carter, until Aronson, M. J. "The Juridical Evolutionism of James Coolidge Carter" in *University of Toronto Law Journal* 10 (1) 1953: 1–53.

Carl von Savigny (1779–1861) also discovered the immeasurable value of custom only when Anton Friedrich Justus Thibaut (1772–1840) proposed in 1814 that all the German lands codify their public and private law on the model of the French *Code civil.*[3] It is characteristic of the differences between civil law and common law legal cultures, that the German debate was conducted by two law professors while the American debate involved two leading advocates at the bar. The rise of the historical school of jurisprudence, both in the German states and in the United States, illustrates G.W.F. Hegel's celebrated observation that "the owl of Minerva takes flight only at dusk." No one had theorized customary law so deeply until legislation and codification threatened to replace it. Indeed, the rise of the historical school cannot be understood apart from its relationship to the rise of Romanticism, historicism, and other aspects of conservative thought. Karl Mannheim famously argued that the first explicit attempts to theorize the nature of historical traditions and to defend the unique value of customary social order (Burke, Maistre, Chateaubriand, Gentz) arose in reaction to the threat posed to all traditions by the French Revolution.[4] Scholars often wonder what happened to the historical school of jurisprudence after Carter. The answer is found already in Carter's Address to the American Bar Association Meeting of 1890: "The Law is a department of sociology."[5] The historical school morphed into legal anthropology and the sociology of law.

Although the historical school of jurisprudence emerged in the wake of the fierce debates provoked by the French Revolution and the *Code civil,* I will examine Carter's theory of custom and customary law in relation to the broader philosophy of social order, from Aristotle to F. A. Hayek.

---

3. For the parallels between the Savigny-Thibaut and the Carter-Field debates on codification, see Reimann, Mathias. "The Historical School Against Codification: Savigny, Carter, and the Defeat of the New York Civil Code" in *The American Journal of Comparative Law* 37 (1) (Winter 1989) 95–119. Stable URL: http://www.jstor.org/stable/840443. And Reimann, *Historische Schule und common law—die deutsche Rechtswissenschaft des 19. Jahrhunderts im amerikanischen Rechtsdenken* (Berlin: Duncker & Humblot, 1993). We know that Carter attended the lectures of Luther Stearns Cushing while he was a student at Harvard Law School (1851–1853). According to Pound, Cushing was "a disciple of Savigny, and was among the first to expound Savigny's doctrines in English." See Pound, "The Ideal and the Actual in Law—Forty-Years After" *The George Washington Law Review* 1 (4) May 1933: 431–447 at 431.

4. Speaking of the historicism of Savigny and Maine, Mannheim says, "Germany achieved for the ideology of conservatism what France did for the Enlightenment—she exploited it to the fullest extent of its logical conclusions." See *From Karl Mannheim*, Ed. Kurt Wolff (New York: Oxford University Press, 1971): 132–222 at 140.

5. Carter "The Ideal and the Actual in the Law" (Philadelphia: Dando Printing, 1890): 22. Carter says that "the philosophy of law" is part of sociology in *Law: Its Origin, Growth, and Function* (New York: G. P. Putnam's Son, 1907) 2.

Several other leading scholars, including Lewis Grossman and Mathias Reimann, have ably discussed Carter's theory of custom and law in the contexts of American legal thought and of European historical jurisprudence. I will instead place Carter's thought, and, by extension, much of the historical school upon which he drew, in the context of the wider philosophical tradition of reflection on custom and social order. Carter was certainly not a great legal philosopher nor even the greatest exponent of the historical school; but his theories have an audacity and a descriptive richness that make them an ideal basis for a philosophical exploration of the theory of custom and customary law. In view of the fact that Carter died before he could revise or finish his major book on legal theory, we must be charitable in how much precision we can expect.[6] Even—or especially—where he is most bold and even simplistic, we find valuable insights and provocations. As one might expect from someone who defends the Gothic meanderings of the common law, Carter's major book is not a model of logical exposition. I have attempted a "restatement," so to speak, of key elements of Carter's thought so that his central claims can be evaluated more accurately. I try to explain Carter, not defend or attack him. H.L.A. Hart says of John Austin that his attempt to reduce all law to the commands of a sovereign accounts for the "half-illuminating, half-obscuring character of his analysis."[7] The same might justly be said of Carter's attempt to reduce all law to custom: reductionism has the virtues of its vices.

Custom has long had a difficult time finding its rightful place among more familiar kinds of social order. Custom is almost always defined by what it is not. Carter also begins his major study of custom and customary law, *Law: Its Origin, Growth, and Function* (1907), by rejecting the two dominant theories of law: the natural law theory and legal positivism. Natural lawyers looked, he said to nature while the positivists looked to deliberate enactment; but Carter argues that law is found in neither of these but in custom.[8] How do we describe a kind of order that is neither

---

6. Lewis Cass Ledyard, the editor of Carter's posthumously published *Law: Its Origin, Growth, and Function*, says in the "prefatory note" that "the rough draft of the manuscript was completed only a few days before he was stricken with the brief illness which resulted in his death. . . . The manuscript had never been finally revised by him. . . ." Despite its unfinished state, LOGF remains the most complete and developed exposition of Carter's mature theory of law, so I rely mainly upon it in my analysis; where I find important amplifications or challenges to the views of LOGF in other writings of Carter, I cite them.

7. Hart, "Introduction" to John Austin, *The Province of Jurisprudence Determined* (London: Weidenfeld and Nicolson, 1954) xi.

8. Carter, *Law: Its Origin, Growth, and Function* [hereafter LOGF] (New York: G. P. Putnam's Son, 1907) 4–6.

natural nor the product of design? Here Carter draws on some ideas both ancient and modern. A great deal of Carter's defense of custom can be seen as an extended commentary on Cicero's eulogy to the wisdom of Roman tradition:

> Cato used to say that the organization of our state surpassed all others for this reason: in others there were generally single individuals who set up the laws and institutions of their commonwealths.... Our commonwealth, in contrast, was not shaped by one man's talent but by that of many; and not in one person's lifetime, but over many generations. He said that there never was a genius so great that he could miss nothing, nor could all the geniuses in the world brought together in one place and at one time foresee all contingencies without the practical experience afforded by the passage of time.... I will have an easier time in completing my task if I show you our commonwealth as it was born, grows up, and comes of age, and as a strong and well-established state, than if I make up some state as Socrates does in Plato.[9]

Carter often quotes Cicero with approval; he never refers to this passage but he should have. Not only does Carter present his theory of customary law in the form of a biography by telling us how custom was born, how it grew up, and how it has now reached scientific maturity, he even echoes Cicero's arguments about the superiority of collective over individual wisdom: "It [custom] is the imperishable record of the wisdom of the illimitable past reaching back to the infancy of the race, revised, corrected, enlarged, open to all alike, and read and understood by all. . . How poor the conclusions of the wisest of lawyers gathered from their own original reflections when compared with those garnered up in the actual customs of life!" (LOGF 127–128).

Carter radicalizes Cato's claims by denying that there ever were the great lawgivers who founded regimes by one supreme act of legislative codification. Cato actually mentions Minos in Crete, Lycurgus in Sparta, Draco and Solon in Athens; only Rome, says Cato, achieved greatness without a supreme original lawgiver. According to Carter, we are all Rome: "There are no Law-givers such as are reverenced in history. Moses, Lycurgus, and Solon took the customs of their time, and gave them form and furnished better methods of securing their enforcement"

[9] Cicero, *De Re Public* II, in Cicero "On the Commonwealth and on the Laws" Ed. James E. G. Zetzel (Cambridge: Cambridge University Press, 1999) 33–34.

(LOGF 49).[10] Of course, historians of law dispute the degree to which the legislation associated with these famous lawgivers reflected custom or not. Finally, Carter also adopts Cato's methodological suggestion to focus on the actual history of law rather than on ideal theories of law. Carter has a thoroughly empirical, even positivistic view of legal science: "science is the orderly arrangement of things we can *know*, and not of things we cannot know. . . " (LOGF 175). And what we can know are observable facts: "Science deals with facts alone, and where there are no facts, there can be no science. . . " (LOGF 13).

Carter argues that both natural law theory and legal positivism fail to provide a scientific basis for the study of law: "In viewing the law as a body of rules proceeding from a supposed Law of Nature—an invisible fountain of right—we are simply indulging in hypothesis. No such thing is open to our observation, and, consequently, not to our knowledge. So too, when we ascribe all law to the command of the supreme power in a State we are simply contenting ourselves with an assumption" (LOGF 13). It is ironic for Austin to be treated as just as unscientific as the natural law theorists, since Austin prided himself on his scientific rigor and poured contempt upon what he saw as the conceptual muddles of the natural law theorists. Carter's point is simply that the Austinian sovereign is pure theoretical construct, just like the principles of natural law. The great legal positivist is accused of failing the test of scientific positivism. Indeed, Carter calls the natural law theory merely "insufficient" while "that of Austin seems to me to be radically and mischievously erroneous" (LOGF 8). Carter's two-fold critique of the natural law theory and of legal positivism rests upon the insight that the legal order depends upon a close connection between right and might. In a strong and just legal order, right is armed with might and might enforces right. But the natural law theory, according to Carter, offers only a vague and theoretical right, while legal positivism offers only amoral might: "And thus while the one tendency would enthrone Right, the other would erect Force, as the arbiter of human conduct" (LOGF 12). Just as good government ought to be both legitimate (*de jure*) and in control (*de facto*), so a good legal system ought to merge right and might.

Carter's defense of custom also draws upon the ancient insight that custom is deeply resistant to deliberate change: when law conflicts with

---

10. Yet, later, Carter praises the greatness of these legislators: "Moses and Solon tower above the great captains of their times" (LOGF 136). Carter's critique of the myth of the ancient lawgivers clearly comes from Alexander Sutherland: "legislators did not exist among the ancients. . . . ancient codes. . . mere compilations of pre-existent custom. . ." See Sutherland, *The Origin and Growth of the Moral Instinct*, 2 vols. (London: Longmans, Green, and Co., 1898) Vol. 2, 170, 176, 180.

custom, custom is likely to prevail, even with the application of massive violence. Hence, as we have seen, Aristotle says that custom is weightier and more authoritative than written law. Thomas Aquinas quotes Isidore with approval that "law ought to be in agreement with the customs of the country" and that "law cannot repress all vices," especially those rooted in custom; Aquinas even says that "custom has the force of law, abolishes law, and is the interpreter of law."[11] Much of Carter's critique of Field or Savigny's critique of Thibaut is captured by Adam Smith's critique of the "man of system":

> The man of system, on the contrary, is apt to be very wise in his own conceit; and is often so enamoured with the supposed beauty of his own ideal plan of government, that he cannot suffer the smallest deviation from any part of it. He goes on to establish it completely and in all its parts, without any regard either to the great interests, or to the strong prejudices which may oppose it. He seems to imagine that he can arrange the different members of a great society with as much ease as the hand arranges the different pieces upon a chess-board. He does not consider that the pieces upon the chess-board have no other principle of motion besides that which the hand impresses upon them; but that, in the great chess-board of human society, every single piece has a principle of motion of its own, altogether different from that which the legislature might chuse to impress upon it. If those two principles coincide and act in the same direction, the game of human society will go on easily and harmoniously, and is very likely to be happy and successful. If they are opposite or different, the game will go on miserably, and the society must be at all times in the highest degree of disorder.[12]

Thus, Carter frequently warns that attempts to enforce laws that conflict with custom "are productive of bribery, perjury, subornation of perjury, animosity and hate among citizens, useless expenditure, and many other public evils. . . it is not so much law as it is tyranny" (LOGF 3). If law were simply the command of the legislature, says Carter, then how do we account for all the statutes that have fallen into desuetude? If a statute can lose its validity by losing the support of custom, then law must acquire its validity from custom in the first place. Carter's insistence that the attempt to use law to suppress custom is either useless or tyrannical leads him to a prescient critique of the growing clamor for temperance laws and to

11. Aquinas, ST I–II, QQ. 95.3 and 96.2.
12. Smith, *Theory of Moral Sentiments*, VI, II, 42.

a disturbing critique of Reconstruction Era legislation aimed at creating political equality for blacks in the South. "Even tyranny may be beneficent in its aims, but never in its results, and the attempt to compel a community of men to right by legislative command, when they do not think it to be right, is tyranny" (LOGF 217). Whatever one thinks of the wisdom of either Prohibition or Reconstruction, Carter is certainly correct in his claims that to attempt to change deep-seated custom by law will often require a huge amount of violence and, even then, likely fail. Carter is often accused by his critics of being merely a poor man's Savigny—that all of Carter's main ideas are found in other masters of historical jurisprudence. I have placed Carter's theory of custom in the context of some ideas of Cicero and Adam Smith to show that even Savigny and Maine can appear derivative in the larger philosophical tradition of thought about custom.

The Moral Foundation of Custom: Liberty

Carter has often been accused by his critics of being more of a natural law theorist than a scientific theorist of customary law[13] and indeed, Carter sometimes sounds like a pure evolutionary positivist and sometimes like a traditional natural lawyer. Lewis Grossman points out that even within the same paragraph, Carter can morph from positivist to moralist: "Science asks primarily only what *is*, not what *ought* to be. So the question here is what, *in fact*, regulates our personal and individual life, not what *ought* to regulate it, although I imagine that the rule which will be found in fact to exist, is the best" (LOGF 145). In Grossman's view, Carter can square his evolutionary positivism with his moral idealism through his confidence that, over time, custom, like the common law, works itself pure.[14] Carter sometimes seems to adopt Edmund Burke's view that what we inherit from tradition has survived the test of time and hence, is likely to be morally good. Grossman rightly argues that Carter was influenced by the evolutionary theory of Alexander Sutherland, whose *The Origin and Growth of the Moral Instinct* (1898) is praised by Carter (LOGF 322). Sutherland develops a Lamarckian theory of the evolution of altruism based on the transmission of acquired characteristics: he tells a story of moral progress

13. Roscoe Pound says of Carter: "While he claims to be a historical jurist, his philosophical position is that of natural law, with individualism and the principles of Anglo-American common law standing for nature." See Pound's review of *Law: Its Origins, Growth, and Function* in *Political Science Quarterly* 24 (2) June 1909: 317–320 at 318.

14. See Grossman "James Coolidge Carter and Mugwamp Jurisprudence," 607–609.

very comforting to Carter.[15] In this story, our natural altruistic instincts, which arose in connect only to our own family, gradually, by repetition and imitation, are strengthened and diffused to wider social circles over time: "We know from physical and moral science that all the acts of man, including his thoughts, have lasting consequences affecting himself. They not only influence his future action, but enter into and modify his physical constitution, and this effect is transmitted to his offspring" (LOGF 126).

A more illuminating way to see how Carter attempts to combine his positivism of custom with his objective theory of morality is to explore Carter's understanding of happiness and liberty. We cannot begin to understand the appeal of custom to Carter until we see the appeal of liberty. Carter, like Aquinas and Bentham, seeks a theory that unites morality and law into a single unified view of human happiness. If happiness is the supreme purpose of individual life, then so must it be the supreme purpose of social and political life. Morality and law must both serve human happiness, each in their own ways. Carter's view of happiness combines elements of Benthamite hedonism with Aristotelian self-actualization over a complete life: "And if life itself is the supreme desire, the largest and completest life must be the nearest approach to pure happiness; not indeed that momentary pleasure which accompanies the activity of any particular desire or passion, but that greatest aggregate sum of pleasures which is the fruit of the activity of all the powers of life" (LOGF 132). Carter then claims that the most important instrument for achieving happiness is liberty: "Liberty, the first of blessings, the aspiration of every human soul, is the supreme object" (LOGF 337). But if liberty is valuable mainly or only as a means to happiness, then why cannot liberty be abridged to better secure happiness? Yet Carter clearly seeks to avoid this obvious threat to liberty in the name of happiness, so he says of liberty: "Every abridgement of it demands an excuse, and the only good excuse is the necessity of preserving it" (LOGF 337). So here Carter in effect demotes happiness and makes liberty the supreme good: "To leave each man to work out in freedom his own happiness or misery" (LOGF 337). What does Carter mean by liberty? Carter defends a perfectly negative conception of liberty: "I define Liberty as being the permission or power to do what one pleases to do without any *external* restraint" (LOGF 133). On Carter's view, liberty is not defined as the positive power to do something but merely as the absence of external constraint. So we are perfectly free on his account

---

15. Unfortunately, Grossman refers to Sutherland's theory as "Darwinian." See Grossman "James Coolidge Carter and Mugwamp Jurisprudence," 609. For Sutherland, see *The Origin and Growth of the Moral Instinct* 2 vols. (London: Longmans, Green, and Co., 1898).

even if incapacitated by superstition and other false beliefs or by illnesses, mental or physical, including addictions. Whatever the defects of Carter's pure theory of negative liberty, it must not be confused with Kant's doctrine: Kant made a very sharp distinction between moral and legal freedom, which Carter rejects.[16]

Carter understands very well that if we seek to maximize negative liberty, then we must minimize external restraint. Of course, to minimize external restraint we must rely upon greater internal restraint: "Self-restraint we must continually exercise, and the practice of it is a means of the highest self-improvement" (LOGF 133). Here is where custom, or more precisely, habit comes to the rescue. For habits make possible an invisible and internal discipline that, unlike the external restraint of law, is compatible with freedom. Carter read this passage in Sutherland: "The action of habit has made the sense of duty automatic."[17] If duty can become spontaneous and automatic, then we can minimize external restraint and maximize freedom. Custom explains why "human conduct is in a very large degree self-regulating. . . . The custom is obeyed unconsciously in most instances because there is no temptation to depart from it, and where the temptation arises self-restraint is exercised through fear of the consequences" (LOGF 15 and 19). So the habitual element of custom is compatible with freedom because it provides an automatic and unconscious internal restraint on conduct: to the extent that I act according to habit, I am perfectly free of external constraint.

By associating custom with liberty, Carter joins a long tradition of thought dating back to Dio Chrysostom: "the laws create a polity of slaves, our customs, on the contrary, create a polity of free men."[18] The external coercion of law seems much less compatible with liberty than the internal restraint of habit. Even Aristotle says that what is habitual is made pleasant. We might well conclude that what we do with pleasure we do freely. And, as we saw, the Roman jurist Julian compared the free consent of custom to the act of voting: by practicing a custom we are freely voting with our deeds. Suárez insists that customs embody the consent of those who practice them. Blackstone also strongly associates custom with liberty: "it is one of the characteristic marks of English liberty, that our common law depends upon custom; which carries this internal evidence of freedom

16. True, Carter himself quotes Kant's definition of law with approval: "The sum total of the conditions under which the personal wishes of one man can be combined with the personal wishes of another man in accordance with a general law of freedom" (LOGF 134). But Carter endorses a unified moral and legal theory of freedom quite contrary to Kant.

17. Sutherland, *The Origin and Growth of the Moral Instinct* 58.

18. Chrysostom, "Discourse 76: Of Custom" Trans. H. Lamar Crosby in *Dio Chrysostom* Vol. 5 (Cambridge: Harvard University Press, 1951) 253 and 255.

along with it, that it probably was introduced by the voluntary consent of the people."[19]

Conduct regulated by custom is also compatible with perfect freedom, according to Carter, because everyone consents to custom: "Customs, therefore, being common modes for action, are the unerring evidence of common thought and belief, and as they are the joint product of the thoughts of all, each one has his own share in forming them. In the enforcement of a rule thus formed no one can complain, for it is the only rule which can be framed which gives equal expression to the voice of each. It restrains only so far as all agree that restraint is necessary. It is the reign of liberty, for it gives to each individual the largest possible area in which he can move and act with unrestricted freedom" (LOGF 143). As we noted in our chapter on Francisco Suárez, the argument that all customs rest on consent is dubious when we consider the many customs of sexual and racial hierarchy. In Carter's account it is not clear how this robust consent is compatible with the unconscious and automatic processes of habit formation. We usually associate consent with explicit and deliberate acts of affirmation. Yet Carter often attributes the learning of customs purely to the unconscious instinct to imitate those around us; he refers to "the obligation felt by each one to do as others do—that is, to conform to custom" (LOGF 18). Carter clearly believes that custom offers a mode of regulating behavior that is uniquely compatible with freedom: first, because customs rest upon the internal and automatic restraints of habit and second, because each of us consents to the normative content of our customs. Perhaps we have no choice whether to consent: in acquiring our customs we unconsciously become who we are and Carter presumes that we have consented to be whoever we actually are.

It is instructive to see in Carter's account how custom and law compare with respect to liberty. Carter does not say that the customary order of conduct involves no external constraints: he compares the sanctions of custom (shame, blame, and ostracism) to the sanctions of law: "the sanctions of each—that is, the forces which compel obedience—are *external*" (LOGF 140). Thus, if both custom and law rely upon external sanctions, wherein lies the unique freedom of custom? First, with law (meaning here legislation), both the norm and its sanctions are external to the agent while with custom, the norm has been internalized. Second, we often resent conforming to a law that we had no part in making while Carter says that each of us has an equal share in the making of custom. So custom rests upon internal consent while law often rests merely upon external sanction.

---

19. Blackstone, *Commentaries on the Laws of England,* Introduction, Sec. 3.

In short, Carter develops a natural law theory of custom. In a natural law theory of law, it is often asserted that "an unjust law is not a law." Carter is not a natural law theorist of custom in this sense: he does not argue that a custom is valid only if it is morally just. Rather, Carter argues that custom itself, as a mode of regulating conduct, is most compatible with liberty, our highest moral ideal. Given his moral libertarianism, Carter has good grounds for arguing that although individual customs may well vary in their moral value, custom as a whole is morally superior to law as a mode of regulating conduct. Carter assumes that custom is always changing and working itself pure; the danger to liberty, and hence, to morality is the replacement of custom as a whole with law. No particular set of customs is sacrosanct for Carter: he assumes that the only thing constant about custom is change. But the order of custom itself, as a mode of human self-regulation, is sacrosanct. Carter is at his most extravagant in praising custom, not when he is focused on particular customs, but when he focuses on the global contrast between legislation and custom: "The former is made by a single human person, or by a very few persons, and necessarily exhibits the imperfection and error which attaches to all such works. The latter is self-existent, eternal, absolutely right and just for the purposes of social government, irrepealable and unchangeable" (LOGF 230–231). Carter's case for the superiority of custom over legislation does not rest upon the superiority of every custom over every statute; it rests upon the superior liberty of custom as a whole over legislation as a whole.

The Moral Foundation of Custom: Utility

Choose your enemies carefully: Carter frequently excoriates the legal theory of Bentham and Austin but he uncritically adopts much of their utilitarian ethics. Carter thus offers two quite different foundations for the morality of custom: liberty and utility. The deepest quandary of Carter's moral defense of custom is how to square his libertarianism with his utilitarianism. He simply does not offer any real guidance for how to reconcile these two ultimate foundations for custom. Like any good legal advocate, he simply multiplies the grounds for defending his client: custom, he argues, maximizes both liberty and utility. He never considers the obvious incompatibilities of these two grounds. Ironically, nowhere is Carter more of a natural law theorist than when he develops a utilitarian justification for custom. Following Austin, Carter attacks the idea of a "moral sense" or faculty of moral intuition. The only moral guide we have is our reason, that is, the judgments of our conscience: "we have no *moral sense* other than conscience, and this is, in fact, only another name for the dictates of reason founded on a view of the consequences of conduct" (LOGF 153). So we have no special faculty for immediately discerning our moral duties; instead, we are stuck with plain old calculative reasoning about the consequences of our conduct. How do we assess the consequences of conduct? From constant study of these consequences, a man "learns that certain kinds of conduct—that is, certain actions—produce pleasure, and that others produce pain. These he classifies and is moved in his conduct to repeat the former and avoid the latter" (LOGF 168). On the basis of these inductive generalizations about pleasure and pain, Carter says that we formulate rules of conduct. He does not explicitly take sides in the dispute between Bentham and Austin about whether the basic unit of the analysis of consequences is a particular act or a rule of conduct. But Carter implicitly seems to side with Austin and adopt a kind of rule utilitarianism in which customs embody the best rules for assessing the balance of pleasure and pain in a course of conduct. Were we to attempt to calculate the net benefits of a particular deed: "life would be the scene of constant perplexity" (LOGF 154). To save us from this morass of utility calculation, we simply rely on custom: when in Rome do as the Romans. A person will quickly discover "that unless he regulates this part of his conduct in accordance with the fair expectations of others, he will suffer punishment of some sort from them, and this supplies an external restraint as a motive to induce him to shape his conduct in accordance with such expectation" (LOGF 169). Still, this external restraint of social sanctions falls short of actual coercion: "Even custom has no power by which it can *compel* a man to do anything" (LOGF 146).

Whereas Austin described our moral sentiments as the precipitate of countless calculations of utility, Carter describes custom as that precipitate: "The habits of our personal lives, like the customs of social life, become the repositories of the numberless conclusions of experience" (LOGF 155). Here we see that Carter does rely upon a kind of Burkean argument that traditional norms are presumptively valid because they have been tested by vast experience: "Manifestly rules thus framed must be superior to any which the wit of particular men could devise. They are not indeed perfect, and as they are the product of average thought, just change as that thought changes" (LOGF 144). Carter, like Burke, asks us to ponder the likelihood that our individual calculation of utility will be superior to the innumerable calculations crystallized in custom.

We can now see that Carter offers both an internalist and externalist account of custom. We discussed his internalist account in connection with his ideal of freedom: on this account, custom maximizes freedom because custom forms our very selves and, by shaping our deepest desires and beliefs, custom regulates our conduct from the inside, so to speak. On this view, custom necessarily rests upon consent of the governed because each of us constantly endorses custom simply by our participation in it. Since custom is not designed or imposed by any determinate person or group, we all create and re-create the customs of our society. This internalist model of spontaneous consent to social order based upon free participation in custom is certainly attractive, but Carter is aware that social order does not rest merely upon such free consensus. Thus, he also develops an externalist account of custom: in this view, we conform to custom, not necessarily because we spontaneously want to, but because we fear the consequences of nonconformity. Carter never explicitly distinguishes these two accounts of custom let alone attempt to reconcile them, but he is faithful enough to the complexity of custom to see that either account by itself is inadequate. Custom cannot persist without a large degree of free consent, but equally custom cannot persist only by free consent; conversely, custom cannot persist only by fear of social sanctions, but equally custom cannot persist without any fear of social sanctions.

What Carter neglects in his discussion of freedom and constraint in custom is the profound asymmetry between an individual and his society. Even if I have an equal share with every other member of society in the creation and maintenance of custom, social custom will always appear to me as an irresistible force. What can one person do to change a social custom? As Shaw said, "The reasonable man adapts himself to the world: the unreasonable one persists in trying to adapt the world to himself. Therefore all progress depends on the unreasonable man." Given the immense asymmetry between any individual and his society, it becomes rational, as Carter says, to conform to custom no matter how perverse those customs are, simply because society is capable of inflicting profound and far-reaching pain upon nonconformists. Why might perverse customs that cause more pain than pleasure persist? Customs based on superstition often suppress many harmless pleasures and customs of sexual, class, or racial hierarchy often inflict a great deal of pain, yet these customs can persist simply because it is rational for any particular individual to conform rather than to incur dreadful moral or legal sanctions. Economists call this phenomenon "adaptive preferences": we rationally tailor what we want based on our judgment of what we are likely to get. Thus, it is only rational for disadvantaged sexes or races to consent to the customs that oppress them. In this way, the external constraint of social sanction becomes internalized as spontaneous consent.

I think it undeniable that, on Carter's account, custom rests upon the morality of objective utility. Yet sometimes Carter seems to defend the converse claim that morality rests simply on custom: "Since conformity to custom is the *necessary* form which human conduct assumes in social dealings, it is the only *just* and *right* form. No other standard can be erected over it" (LOGF 131). In support of this positivism of custom, Carter also sometimes denies that there could be such a thing as a bad custom.[20] Now Carter acknowledges that common law courts do sometimes declare customs to be bad and refuse to give them legal effect (LOGF 80). But Carter says that these supposed "bad customs" were not actually customs at all: "Thefts are extremely frequent, but they are, like all crimes, departures from custom—mere bad *practices* which true custom condemns" (LOGF 80). Carter gives the example of an action against a milkman for watering his milk; the milkman defends himself on the grounds that watering milk is the custom among milkmen.[21] Interestingly, Carter denies that this practice is a custom on the grounds that it is done secretly: "The act was done in secret with the view of concealing it from customers" (LOGF 81). Is Carter's distinction between a custom and a bad practice merely a sophism designed to support his claim that there are no bad customs?[22] Carter defends his distinction on the basis that custom rests upon what philosophers today call "common knowledge." Carter calls this common knowledge "reciprocal fair expectation": "Custom is the one thing that all may safely be presumed to know" (LOGF 191). As we discussed earlier, philosophers agree that common knowledge is the basis of all conventions. Common knowledge means that not only that every participant in a convention knows the convention, but also every participant knows that every other participant knows the convention: I know the convention, I know that you know the convention, and I know that you know that I know the convention. So if all customs are also conventions, then customs must also rest upon this kind of common knowledge. Now clearly among milkmen and their customers there was no such common knowledge of watering

20. Already in "The Ideal and the Actual in Law," Carter claims that so-called bad customs are "not customs, but violations of custom" (20).

21. Carter's example here of a creative use of custom as a defense is quite similar to a later actual case of car salesmen who appealed to custom to defend their practice of turning back odometers on used cars.

22. Grossman thinks so: "Carter played semantic games, terming them 'bad practices' rather than 'customs'." See Grossman, "Langdell Upside Down," 159.

milk. The more interesting question is whether among milkmen there was genuine common knowledge of this practice?[23] If there were common knowledge among milkmen, then one can rightly say that there was a custom among milkmen of watering the milk. Is this custom among milkmen of watering the milk a bad custom? Not at all: there is nothing bad about diluting milk. What makes it bad is to use it to defraud customers, but we have already seen that there was no custom among milkmen and their customers to water the milk. So Carter turns out to be right that selling diluted milk is not a bad custom but merely a bad practice. Of course, this one example falls far short of proving that there are no bad customs.[24]

Despite Carter's success at sometimes showing that what are called bad customs are not customs at all, Carter is not deeply committed to the claim that all custom is good. He is only committed to the much weaker claim that all custom is presumptively good: "While conscience informs us that we should, in general obey the law and custom. . . still its own final command is supreme over both custom and law" (LOGF 151–152).[25] So Carter does, in the end, erect a moral standard over custom. His view that custom is likely to be a safer guide to conduct than one's own fallible judgment is certainly compatible with the view that custom itself is not infallible. Carter's claims are thus often hedged: "Whatever custom pronounces to be just, conscience in general accepts and declares to be right" (LOGF 163). Carter's ethics are coherent in the sense that both custom and conscience are justified in their rules to the extent that those rules accurately reflect the true calculus of utility. Indeed, Carter is sharply critical of Alexander Hamilton for subordinating his conscience to the custom of dueling.[26]

Consensus and Conflict in the Evolution of Custom and Law

What can we learn about custom from Carter's history of law? Every theory of law acknowledges the role of both consensus and conflict, but

---

23. "This surely, even were it a custom of milkmen generally—and I impute to that class no such dishonesty—is not the custom of men in general." Carter, "The Ideal and the Actual," 20.

24. Later, in an aside, Carter again claims that bad customs are merely bad practices (LOGF 122).

25. Carter says this several times: "conscience as the ultimate governor of our entire conduct has a supervisory jurisdiction over the commands of custom and even of law" (LOGF 165).

26. "Alexander Hamilton gave a pathetic picture of the struggle between these rival sentiments [custom and conscience] when, having on many previous occasions borne his testimony against the practice of dueling. . . " (LOGF 166). True, Carter does not call dueling a custom here, but it clearly fits all his definitions of custom and the context here is about the conflict between custom and conscience.

some theories of law emphasize consensus and other theories emphasize conflict. In consensus theories, law serves to articulate and to enforce the shared norms of the society; in conflict theories, law serves to resolve disputes that arise from the absence of consensus. In general, conflict theories of law will emphasize the difference between law and custom whereas consensus theories of law will emphasize the similarity of law to custom. Savigny developed a consensus theory of law: he compared law to language because law also articulates what a nation has in common: "this organic connection of law with the being and character of the people. . . it may be compared with language. . . Law grows with the growth, and strengthens with the strength of the people, and finally dies away as the nation loses its nationality." Savigny says that like language, law defines the unique genius of each nation: "the common consciousness of the people is the peculiar seat of law."[27] For Savigny, custom is not law; rather custom is merely evidence or a sign of law: "Custom therefore is the badge and not a ground of origin of positive law."[28] Like language, law evolves "by internal silently-operating powers, not by the arbitrary will of a law-giver."[29] Only at a later stage, says Savigny, do grammarians develop a science of language and jurists a science of law. Although Savigny does not say so, we can interpret the rise of grammarians and of jurists with the rise of conflict: these experts are needed only when there is disagreement about language or law. By contrast, Henry Sumner Maine develops a conflict theory of law: "When a king decided a dispute by a sentence, the judgment was assumed to be the result of direct inspiration. The divine agent, suggesting judicial awards to kings or to gods, the greatest of kings, was *Themis*." Maine thus argues that divine judgment, not custom, is the origin of law: "However strongly we, with our modern associations, may be inclined to lay down *a priori* that the notion of a Custom must precede that of a judicial sentence, and that a judgment must affirm a Custom or punish its breech, it seems quite certain that the historical order of the ideas is that in which I have placed them"[30] Later, in his *Early History of Institutions*, Maine emphasizes custom more than divine judgment: "Outside each threshold is immemorial custom blindly obeyed;

---

27. Savigny, *The Vocation of Our Age for Legislation and Jurisprudence*, Trans. Abraham Hayward (London: Littlewood and Co.) 27–28.
28. Savigny, *System of the Modern Roman Law*, Trans. William Holloway. Vol. 1. (Westport, CT: Hyperion Press, 1980) 28.
29. Savigny, *The Vocation of Our Age for Legislation and Jurisprudence* 30.
30. Maine, *Ancient Law* (1861) 3 and 4.

inside is the Patria Potestas exercised by a half-civilized man over wife, child, and slave."[31]

In his history of custom and law, Carter weaves together both the themes of consensus and of conflict. Custom, he says, rests upon a consensus among the living and between the living and the dead: "It is important to observe that the establishment of a custom takes time, and long periods of time, and as all conduct is preceded by thought, it also involves a long series of similar thoughts—that is, of long-concurring common opinion" (LOGF 19–20). Carter's emphasis here upon the long-standing nature of custom contrasts with his innovative doctrine developed later. In traditional common law doctrine, custom generally has legal force only if it has existed "time immemorial"; but Carter rightly claims that what matters for the legal force of custom is not its age but its function as a coordinating convention today: "*Ancient* customs they have indeed regarded as having the force of law, but his quality they impute, not to the custom, *qua* custom, but to its *antiquity*, whereas the conclusion at which I arrive erects *present existing* custom as the standard of law" (LOGF 121).[32] In short, the agreement that matters for the legal force of custom today is the agreement of the community today. Yet Carter is well aware that customary consensus never lasts forever, but he denies that the emergence of conflict and tribunals changes the legal force of custom: "What is demanded at this stage of human progress is, not some new *law*, for the conception even of legislation does not as yet exist, but some properly qualified *judge*, and some method of compelling the appearance of an adversary before him—that is to say, a *method of procedure*" (LOGF 31). Carter rightly insists that the basis for such dispute resolution must be the interpretation and application of the existing custom: "An existing dispute between men must, of necessity, consist of a difference of opinion concerning the *conduct* which one is *entitled to expect* from the other, and the expectation of either party can be justified only by an appeal to what he supposes to be the *existing* rule or custom applicable to the case. Neither party will assert a *new* rule, for that would, of itself, condemn him" (LOGF 31).

But simply because a tribunal has affirmed an existing custom in its judgment does not mean that something significant has not happened in the relationship of custom to law. As Carter should know from the nature

31. Maine, *Lectures on the Early History of Institutions* (New York: Henry Holt, 1875) 393.

32. John Chipman Gray applauds this innovation of Carter: "And on this point Mr. Carter's theory seems an improvement on Blackstone's. . . so far as custom is a source of the Law as it now exists, it is present custom." *The Nature and Sources of the Law* 2nd ed. (Gloucester, MA: Peter Smith, 1972) 284.

of the common law, when courts apply existing norms to new disputes, the norms themselves change. The application of old norms is always, willy-nilly, creative of new norms. Moreover, even in those cases in which the old norm has not been applied to a new case, the existing social norm has now been doubly institutionalized: first in customary practice and now in a court. As legal anthropologist Paul Bohannan puts it, "All institutions (including legal institutions) develop customs. Some customs, in some societies, are reinstitutionalized at another level: they are restated for the more precise purposes of legal institutions. When this happens, therefore, law may be regarded as a custom that has been restated in order to make it amenable to the activities of the legal institutions."[33] Now Carter is aware that his *bête noir*, John Austin, had already argued that customs do not become law until recognized and applied by courts. No doubt Carter would say that the reason courts enforce the customs they do is because they consider them to be already binding law. If courts created new law by enforcing customs, then they would be applying that law retroactively upon the parties to the current dispute.

Still, Carter has his own reasons for wanting to mark the distinction between custom and law: "But while all Law is Custom, all Custom is not necessarily Law. Law differs from Custom as a part differs from the whole" (LOGF 120). So how do we know what part of custom counts as law? Carter rejects Austin's theory that custom is but a source of law: "as if there were some governmental power standing above custom, the function of which was to pronounce judgment on the wisdom of custom, and select from it the rules it would enforce and reject the rest" (LOGF 121). Yet by Carter's own theory, since not all custom is law, there must be some institution responsible for deciding what part of custom shall be enforced by law. Carter observes that many violations of custom are punished by moral sanction and social ostracism rather than by legal sanctions. But Carter is aware that what counts as a violation of etiquette in some societies is treated as a crime in others, so is there any general criterion by which to distinguish mere custom from legal custom? All customs create what Carter calls "fair expectation," and thus every violation of custom creates disappointed expectations, so mere disappointment cannot be the basis of legal custom. Ultimately, for Carter, the difference between mere custom and legal custom is a question of the degree of disappointment: "Where violations of custom are calculated to excite such irritation and displeasure

---

33. Paul Bohannan, "The Differing Realms of the Law" in *Law and Warfare*, Ed. Paul Bohannan (Garden City, NY: The Natural History Press, 1967) 43–56, at 47.

as to provoke violence and perhaps bloodshed they are destructive of society, and the repression of them becomes necessary to social existence" (LOGF 139). Carter's extended discussion of the law of marine insurance might offer some refinements to his notions of the role of expectations and disappointments in custom and law. In a dispute between a ship owner and an insurance underwriter, Carter considers a hypothetical case in which the ship owner violates a custom by not disclosing to the underwriter all the risks material to his insurance policy. However, in this case, the underwriter happened to have already had the relevant knowledge of risk, despite the concealment by the ship owner. Carter argues that in this case, the underwriter has no legal claim against the ship owner because he evidently did not rely upon the concealment of the ship owner and, hence, cannot be said to have been harmed by that reliance. However, had the underwriter relied upon the ship owner's failure to disclose, then he would have been harmed by that concealment. So mere violation of customary expectations does not create law: only violations of customary expectations that involve reliance and actual harm can be actionable at law (LOGF 70–74, 271–278). Of course, it is precisely where we have reliance and harm that disputes over custom are most likely to turn violent, thus creating the need to enforce them as law.

Turning from the private law of contracts and torts to the public law of crime, Carter makes the same essential point: "All crimes are violations of custom, but all violations of custom are not necessarily crimes" (LOGF 241). So what kinds of violations of custom count as crimes in law? Here we find the same rule as before: "The function of the criminal law is to preserve society from violence, for violence is war, and threatens the existence of society" (LOGF 242). But Carter blurs this simple rule whereby legal custom is that subset of custom whose violation will likely lead to violence when he says. "Now, as there is no test of right and wrong in the law save custom, *mala in se* are simply palpable violations of custom, while the converse expression *mala prohibita*, indicates acts which the law makes criminal without regard to custom" (LOGF 243–242). But if there are crimes "without regard to custom," then what about Carter's claim that "all crimes are violations of custom"? As we shall see below, this is only the beginning of the problems that Carter creates for himself by denying that custom can be evaluated by morality or law.

Now that we have seen Carter attempt to distinguish custom from law, we can also see that for him custom rests upon consensus but that law rests upon conflict. Custom, like language, is what we share in common: "Inasmuch as the constitutions of men in the same society are similar and the environments similar, the thoughts must be similar and the conduct consequently similar. Hence human conduct necessarily presents itself in the form of similarity—habits and customs" (LOGF 123).[34] And Carter explicitly says that custom creates harmony: "Custom is effectual only when it is universal, or nearly so. In the absence of unanimity of opinion, custom becomes powerless, or rather does not exist" (LOGF 38). But of course, customs are interpreted differently by different people, leading to conflict over custom: all conflict rests upon shared understandings, and shared customs create lots of conflict. Sometimes Carter concedes that custom itself, as opposed to conflicting interpretations of custom, can be unsettled and at odds with itself: "in early and rude societies. . . customs, in many respects are not settled and are in conflict. A judicial decision determines them so far as it extends" (LOGF 66). "This arbitration of quarrels is a near approach to the establishment of a court" (LOGF 48). So, conflict over custom leads to the declaration of legal custom by tribunals of various kinds. Custom arises from cooperation while law arises from conflict. When conflict over custom becomes deeply divisive and intractable, then we see the emergence of legislation. Carter traces the rise of the XII Tables in Rome and Solon's Code in Athens to the need to impose a political settlement upon two societies polarized by class warfare: "the object, substance, and nature of those written laws was not *juristic*, but *political*" (LOGF 88). Indeed, Carter sees not only the origin of legislation in class warfare, but he even concedes that in his own Gilded Age America the battle between labor and capital had become so bloody that a legislative settlement may have to be imposed: "The office of legislation is to permit this war to be carried through to its result, but without violence" (LOGF 261). In short, although Carter sees custom as the essential and invisible glue holding together a community, he recognizes that conflict between customs and over customs creates the need for courts and legislatures. Law remedies the deficiencies of custom.

Custom: Usage or Opinion?

Carter's discussion whether custom is a matter of sheer objective usage or is also a matter of subjective (personal or public) opinion reveals the

34. "Customs, therefore, being common modes of action, are the unerring evidence of common thought and belief. . . " (LOGF 143); "The prime requisite of human society, that without which it cannot subsist, is that each member should know what to expect in the conduct of others, and that fair expectations should not be disappointed. . . This requirement is supplied by conformity to custom" (LOGF 18).

hazards of attempting sharply to distinguish usage from conviction in custom. The relation of thought to action is complex and puzzling in the case of custom. To the extent that custom rests upon automatic habit, one might say that it represents almost pure action and little thought. Yet all customs embody social conventions and they depend crucially upon the common knowledge of those conventions. Carter is not always consistent in what he says about thought and action in custom. "The simplest definition of custom is that it is *uniformity of conduct* of all persons under like circumstances" (LOGF 122–123). So what is conduct? Sometimes Carter defines conduct in purely physical terms: "*Conduct* is some *physical movement* of the body, and is invariably preceded by some *thought* or *feeling* which is its *cause*" (LOGF 123). Whether one can define any example of conduct without recourse to issues of motive, purpose, or intention is not a question Carter explicitly considers, though he often describes conduct, not in physical terms, but in terms of intentions and motives.[35] Indeed, sometimes Carter seems to define custom more in terms of thought than in terms of conduct: "Customs, therefore, being common modes of action, are the unerring evidence of common thought and belief" (LOGF 143). Here action is merely evidence of thought. Carter sometimes associates custom with opinion more than with action: "In the absence of unanimity of opinion, custom becomes powerless, or rather does not exist" (LOGF 38). And elsewhere he says, "Who does not know that the ultimate support upon which all laws must rest is public opinion?"[36]

John Chipman Gray takes Carter to task for confusing custom with opinion: "*Customary opinion* is an incorrect expression. Custom is what men *do*, not what they *think*."[37] Gray points out that our opinion about what ought to be done is often quite different from what we do: custom refers to what we actually do, not what we think or say. Most people might agree that lying is almost always wrong, but is it not customary in many contexts to always tell the truth. Gray asks, "Is the opinion of his community on a question of morality, of right and wrong, not yet embodied in practice, a

35. "Conduct consists in some physical movement of the body, and it is of such movements only that the law takes direct notice, although in some exceptional cases where the nature of an act is qualified by the intention which prompts it, it may inquire as to that intention" (LOGF 167). But if consequences are all that matter to moral evaluation, as Carter frequently asserts, then why should we take any notice of intentions? Carter also says: "The motive to all action is to enjoy pleasure or to avoid pain" (LOGF 167–168). So on his account, either intentions or motives or both are built into the very notion of action or conduct.

36. Carter, *The Proposed Codification of Our Common Law* (Whitefish, MT: Kessinger Publishing: 2010) 41.

37. Gray, *The Nature and Sources of the Law* 285.

legitimate source of Law to which a judge ought to subordinate his own opinion?" Then Gray answers, "I know of no moralist or jurist who has answered the question in the affirmative."[38] Gray clearly does not know many jurists of customary international law. In the formal doctrine of customary international law, a custom has legal force only if it combines actual practice (*usus*) with the belief that the practice is legally binding (*opinio iuris*). Customary international law must combine both of these elements, but how belief and practice jointly constitute custom is the subject of robust debate among lawyers. For example, many norms of international justice such as prohibitions on military intervention and on torture are violated frequently in practice but asserted frequently in resolutions of the United Nations and other multinational bodies. Do these norms, more often preached than practiced, count as customary law? How much compliance with a norm counts as usage? How many official declarations count as conviction of legal necessity? In an influential analysis, Frederic Kirgis argues that international tribunals have adopted a sliding scale in weighing the role of both practice and conviction. Where there is lots of evidence of consistent state practice (*usus*), there is little need for evidence of belief in legal obligation (*opinio iuris*); conversely, where there is lots of evidence of belief in legal obligation, there is little need for evidence of consistent state practice.[39] With respect to customary international law, then, the strongest evidence for custom is when consistent state practice is reinforced by consistent declarations of legal obligation, but custom can also gain legal force by practice alone or by declaration of obligation alone. So Carter's ambivalence about the importance of both opinion and conduct in the determination of custom is well justified in the arena of international law.

We Know More Than We Can Say: Why All Law Is Custom

Carter is perhaps most famous (or rather infamous) for his statement: "All Law is Custom" (LOGF 120). Often, his whole theory of custom and customary law is simply reduced to this slogan and dismissed. A similar strategy is often used to summarize and then dismiss the natural law theory of Thomas Aquinas, reduced to the slogan "an unjust law is not a law." In both cases, these slogans are on the surface deeply misleading and can

---

38. Gray, *The Nature and Sources of the Law* 290.

39. Frederic L. Kirgis, "Custom on a Sliding Scale," in *The American Journal of International Law* 81 (1) Jan. 1987: 146–151.

be understood only after a detailed and comprehensive study of the whole theory. Jurists in the Roman law tradition often distinguished several independent sources of law (*fontes iuris*), of which custom was only one. And Blackstone divides the law of England into common law and statute. More recently, H.L.A. Hart offers a rule of recognition for identifying English law: "Statute or consistent with statute." So whether we follow traditional or contemporary jurists, Carter's claim that all law is custom seems both simplistic and false. Carter often accused John Austin of reducing all law to legislation by defining law as the command of a sovereign. So Carter seems to be offering his own counter-reduction of law to custom. Of course, students of Carter know that he strongly distinguishes law from legislation (LOGF 229), so Carter cannot be accused of the strikingly novel claim that legislation is actually custom.[40] As for common law, Blackstone had already defined common law as "general custom," so Carter's slogan at one level is simply a flashback to pre-Benthamite English jurisprudence.

At a deeper level, however, Carter is making a more radical and startling claim. What Carter ultimately means by "all law is custom" is that "all law is the custom of the court." To make sense of that claim, let us first turn to a related argument by John Chipman Gray, who famously argued that both custom and statutes were merely sources of law. By "sources," he really meant raw material: Gray argues that we don't know the precise meaning of either customs or statutes until we see their bearing on actual conduct—that is, until a court interprets and applies the sources to live controversies. Until courts produce a "finished product," namely, a precise formulation of a rule deciding a case, we cannot really know what the law means. In Gray's argument, neither custom nor statutes are self-interpreting, and until they receive authoritative interpretation in a court, we do not actually know what they mean. Thus, Grey identifies law with the finished product of judicial interpretation and application: "Rules of conduct laid down and applied by the courts of a country are coterminous with the Law of that country." Gray defends this definition of law by quoting Bishop Hoadly: "Whoever hath an absolute authority to interpret any written or spoken laws, it is he who is truly the Law-giver to all intents and purposes, and not the person who first wrote or spoke them."[41]

---

40. In correspondence, Grossman points out that in "The Ideal and the Actual," (14), where Carter does not distinguish law from legislation, Carter comes close to saying that legislation is custom. Speaking of statutes, Carter says: "if it be habit, custom, and opinion alone which give to commands the force of law, it follows that the real substance of the law is not the command, but the habit, custom and opinion which it embodies."

41. Gray, *The Nature and Sources of the Law* 102.

Now Carter agrees with Gray that law ought to be identified with the activity of courts. Following Savigny, Carter argues that although custom was once found in the usages of ordinary people, over time the development of legal custom has been entrusted to lawyers: the *Volksrecht* has given way to the *Juristenrecht*: "The body of custom therefore, tends from the beginning to become a harmonious system. When the ascertainment and administration of custom are committed in enlightened society to learned judges, who are men of science, improvement becomes more rapid and certain, but the process is the same" (LOGF 331–332).[42] So whatever Carter means by "all law is custom," he clearly identifies law with the activity of courts.[43]

Notice, however, that Gray identifies the activity of courts with "rules of conduct laid down" while Carter identifies courts with custom. Traditionally, the law that emerged from the activities of courts was called "unwritten" in contrast to the "written" law of legislation. As Blackstone observes, the common law is styled "unwritten" not because it resides in an oral tradition, but because it rests upon the usages of the court and of the realm. Bentham often observed sarcastically that the unwritten law fills whole libraries. Gray has lost sight of the sense in which the activity of courts is unwritten when he defines that activity as "rules of conduct laid down by courts": here the activity of courts is reduced to laying down explicit rules, much like a legislature. Indeed, Gray misses a crucial distinction between legislatures and courts: whereas statutory rules get their authority from once being "laid down," the rules of common law acquire their authority from being "taken up" by subsequent judges. So whereas Blackstone and Carter identify the activity of courts with usage and custom, Gray identifies it with explicit written rules.

Why does it matter whether we characterize the activity of courts in terms of customs or rules? Because that is what is at stake in the debate over the codification of the common law. If the activity of the courts can be adequately described in terms of "rules of conduct laid down," then there can be little objection to the project of collecting and organizing all those rules (*rationes decidendi*) into an authoritative code. By contrast, the

---

42. On Savigny see Reimann, "The Historical School Against Codification," 110. Carter already marked the transition from the people's law to the lawyers' law in his book *The Proposed Codification of Our Common Law* 5.

43. Grossman argues that "Carter's legal science was not nearly so autonomous as Savigny's, let alone Puchta's. With increasing frequency as the years passed, Carter maintained that judges should refer directly to societal customs as well as to judicial precedents." See Lewis A. Grossman, "From Savigny through Sir Henry Maine": Roscoe Pound's Flawed Portrait of James Coolidge Carter's Historical Jurisprudence (American University, WCL Research Paper No. 2009-21) 11.

ancient maxim of Roman law says, "*lex curiae est cursus curiae.*" Here is Carter's theory of law: law is the custom of the court. We saw earlier that custom is the intersection of convention and habit. If law is based in the custom of the court, then law involves both explicit conventions and the tacit know-how of habitual conduct. The law of the court is more than the explicit rules it formulates. And if knowledge of law is significantly rooted in the tacit professional habits of lawyers and judges, then the activities of courts cannot be reduced to written rules. In short, Carter's fundamental argument against codification is we lawyers and judges know more about law than we can say: knowledge of law involves more than explicit rules. No code can possibly capture the tacit wisdom of legal professionals in identifying, interpreting, and applying norms to disputes.[44]

Unfortunately, on the key issue of the relationship between knowledge and writing, Carter in his book fumbles badly. Carter rightly says that David Dudley Field's argument for a code rests fundamentally on this claim: "First: Whatever is clearly *known*, can be clearly *stated in writing*, and therefore, all that is clearly known of law can be clearly stated in writing" (LOGF 270).[45] Amazingly, Carter simply yields the primary field of battle to Field: "The first proposition is a mere truism. Who has ever doubted the possibility or expediency or reducing our knowledge of that law, as of everything else, to writing?" (LOGF 270–271). Here as elsewhere in his book, Carter shows himself in thrall to his archenemy Bentham. Yet Carter clearly knows better: "The especial champions of written law are indeed obliged to admit that *all* law cannot be reduced to writing; for, after it is written, it must still be interpreted and applied, and such interpretation necessarily involves a resort to unwritten rules."[46]

---

[44] For a study of the tacit and habitual know-how of experts, including lawyers, see Schwartz, Barry and Kenneth Sharpe *Practical Wisdom* (New York: Riverhead Books, 2010). What Pound says of Carter is true of all defenses of "insider" know-how: "As had been true of the historical school before him, he assumes that the received ideals of the profession are identical with those of the community." Pound, "The Ideal and the Actual In Law, Forty Years After," 445.

[45] For Field's words, see his "Codification—Mr. Field's Answer to Mr. Carter" in *American Law Review* 24 (1890): 255–266 at 260: "Cannot the general rules of law, relating to these subjects, so far as they are already settled and established rules of decision, be stated in writing? We know they can."

[46] Carter, *The Provinces of the Written and the Unwritten Law* (New York: Banks and Brothers, 1889) 6. Carter adopts a more nuanced critique of Field in *The Proposed Codification of our Common Law*: "The fallacy (and it is a gross one), wrapped up in these plausible assertions that whatever is know can be written, and that if a rule can be written by a judge in an opinion, it can be written and enacted in a Code, consists in the false assumption that courts lay down rules *absolutely*, whereas, they lay them down *provisionally* only" (25).

What need is there of any tradition of common law legal reasoning if the whole of our knowledge of law could be reduced to writing? In defense of Carter, it should be said that only after Ludwig Wittgenstein did philosophers come to appreciate the importance of the fundamental truth that we all know much more than we can say. Wittgenstein famously showed that there can be no complete set of rules for how to follow a rule without an infinite regress. What this means for law is that there can be no complete set of explicit rules for how to identify, interpret, or apply a rule of law without an infinite regress.[47] Later, Gilbert Ryle showed that there is a fundamental difference between knowing how and knowing that: knowing that something is a legal rule does not mean knowing how to interpret or apply it. Michael Oakeshott, Michael Polanyi, F. A. Hayek, and many others argued in a variety of contexts that our practical, tacit, and personal know-how cannot be reduced to written codes. The traditional description of the common law as "unwritten"—despite Bentham's abuse—is a definitional truth. Carter should have realized that common law is not unwritten merely by accident: common law is essentially unwritten.

After surrendering the main defense of the common law to Field, Carter takes his stand on the much less important distinction between *stating* a law and *enacting* it, that is, on the difference between a digest or restatement of law and a legislative imposition of a code. But in explaining this distinction, Carter tacitly acknowledges the distinction between knowing how and knowing that. Carter says that by merely stating a law, we leave it open to the lawyer or judge to use his tacit know-how in deciding how to apply that stated rule to analogous cases in the future: "*Stating* a rule of the common unwritten law is putting into words a rule by which all conduct of the kind described may, so far as the past enables us to determine, be governed consistently with the sense of justice, but which future experience may require to be restricted, amended, or enlarged" (LOGF 271). What Carter is arguing here is that mere digests or restatements of law do not attempt to capture the whole of law but presuppose the necessity of a background of shared tacit understandings about how to identify cases that fall under the rule as well as how to apply this rule "with a sense of justice."

These capacities, identifying relevant cases and applying the rule justly, obviously rest upon tacit know-how quite independent of the digest or restatement. Carter also assumes that the digest or restatement leaves open

---

47. "We may indeed enact rules of interpretation; but these must themselves be interpreted. . . " Carter, "Provinces of the Written and Unwritten Law," 6.

the exact formulation the relevant rule, so that it can be reformulated by restriction or enlargement in the future. By contrast, Carter says of a legislated code: "*Enacting* a rule of the common law is *making* an absolute rule by which all such conduct *must* be governed, regardless of the sense of justice" (LOGF 271). Instead of presupposing a body of tacit knowledge among lawyers using a code, the code attempts to lay down an exact formulation of the rule in the hope of thereby capturing all or most of the tacit know-how of those applying code. Where they operate under a code, courts are not permitted to reformulate the rule so as to fit the facts of new cases: no matter how different the new cases, the exact same rule must be applied. In this way, courts are prevented from using their tacit "sense of justice" to revise the rules as the cases evolve. Carter points to the fundamental dilemma facing every drafter of a codified rule: if the rule is framed narrowly and precisely, then it will be a Procrustean bed for future cases and lead to absurdity and injustice; if the rule is framed broadly and generally, then it provides too little guidance for future conduct. Narrow rules are too certain while broad rules are too uncertain. Carter's emphasis on the need to reformulate the rules of the common law in the light of new cases shows his awareness that common law is not a matter of applying fixed rules to changing facts; rather, as the facts change, so must the rules. Common law is a moving system of classification in which the categories and the cases evolve together.[48] Although Carter fumbles badly in conceding that everything known can be stated in writing, he recovers the ball of his claims by arguing that the use of digests necessarily taps into the deep reservoirs of practical wisdom in lawyers leading to better and more nuanced decisions. In the end, "all law is custom" means "we common lawyers know more than we can say."

Carter was no common law fanatic: he acknowledged the necessity for legislation to revoke and to replace some key traditions of common law doctrine. Common law evolves, but not fast enough in the unprecedented conditions of modern society. Carter says that the traditional doctrine of coverture could not be accommodated to the economic and political equality of women just as the traditional doctrine of master and servant could not be accommodated to the conditions of modern industry (LOGF 259–260). But Carter never considered the possibility that there might be a deep conflict within his own society between the ideals of lawyers and the ideals of ordinary citizens. Carter's defense of the practical wisdom of lawyers and judges presumes that we citizens can trust them to

48. See Carter, *The Proposed Codification of our Common Law* 25–26.

articulate and to protect our own cherished practices and the beliefs that sustain them. What Roscoe Pound says of Carter is true of all defenses of "insider" know-how: "As had been true of the historical school before him, he assumes that the received ideals of the profession are identical with those of the community."[49] Common law works best where customs of economic and social life are genuinely common.

---

49. Pound, "The Ideal and the Actual in Law," 445.

EPILOGUE: CUSTOM AND LAW

ALTHOUGH THIS BOOK IS titled *The Philosophy of Customary Law*, we have been more focused on custom than on customary law. Our philosophers of law rightly understand that the puzzles about customary law arise mainly because of inadequate conceptions of custom. I have not attempted to solve all of the major puzzles about customary law, but I hope that this book will contribute to their solution. Nor will I attempt here to summarize the insights of Aristotle, Suárez, Bentham, and Carter. In each of the chapters, I have emphasized how each of our thinkers was responding to the claims of his predecessors. Their ideas form a dialectic that would be tedious to rerun here. Instead, I will simply offer a few reflections about the nature of custom and of the relation of custom to law, building on what we have learned from these philosophers of law and contemporary jurists.

What is the relation of custom to morality? With the partial exception of Bentham, our philosophers agree that customs are intelligible only in relation to basic norms of objective morality or natural law. That customs could be grounded in objective morality seems at first implausible since, presumably, moral norms are permanent and universal while customs are transient and local. But, following David Lewis, when we see that customs embody social conventions and that most conventions are coordinating principles, we also see that there are innumerably many ways to coordinate human conduct toward the same set of morally justified goods. Hence, the same goods of marriage, friendship, knowledge, play, skilled work, religion, and beauty can be pursued by an infinitely wide array of coordinating conventions. A morally conscientious person who seeks to participate in these goods realizes that he must coordinate his conduct with his fellows. He notices that his society has its own coordinating conventions, starting with a common language. So he adopts these conventions (or grows into them). Thus, if we wish to participate in the basic goods of human life, shared with other members of a particular historical community, then we are required, in many contexts, to adopt common customs. There is often no possible way to enjoy these goods apart from those coordinating conventions. Insofar as customs truly facilitate the enjoyment of genuine human goods, they are consistent with objective morality.

Customs can undermine true morality in two ways: they can lead us to false goods and they can arbitrarily frustrate the enjoyment of true goods. In the first way, Aquinas says that the ancient Germans had customs that encouraged theft; and today, we have customs that encourage gambling and gun violence. Customs of gender and racial hierarchy arbitrarily frustrate the enjoyment of true goods by subordinated groups: often women or persons of color have had their opportunities for pursuing basic goods arbitrarily restricted. Still, these important exceptions notwithstanding, most customs have always been consistent with the pursuit of the genuine goods identified by true morality.

Seeing customs as coordinating principles also enables us to see why people are often led to conform to customs that they resent or even hate. As we saw in our discussion of Suárez and of Carter, many people conform to customs they resent both because they fear ostracism and because even hated customs make available many social goods. Many colonized peoples adopt the hated language of their oppressors, purely because of the need for a lingua franca. Better to speak the oppressors' tongue than not to be able to communicate at all with one's rulers. Similarly, subjugated minorities often adopt hated customs of deference: better to bow to one's "superiors" than not to be able to work or to marry. It is perfectly rational to value the basic goods of human life more than the content of the particular conventions that enable us to enjoy them. In short, there are many sound reasons to think that people often conform to customs without consenting to them in any way.

Custom will relate to law in very different ways depending upon whether we focus on the lay customs of popular conduct or on the professional customs of lawyers. Many disputes about the relation of custom to law stem from a failure to distinguish these two very different kinds of customs. For example, most jurists list custom as one among several independent sources of law, but the jurists of the historical school often assert that all law is custom.[1] How could all law be custom if custom is but one source of law? If we focus on lay customs, then custom is but one source of our legal conventions; but if we focus on lawyerly customs, then all law rests upon custom, in the sense that the interpretation and application of all law rest upon those lawyerly customs.

But beneath this familiar contrast of lay and lawyerly custom is a deeper contrast between the conventional and the habitual dimensions of custom. Both lay customs and the customs of lawyers have a conventional and a habitual dimension. Lay customs are related to law primarily as one source of conventions adopted into legal rules. The customs of merchants are a good example of conventions as a source of the law merchant. Whether or to what extent those lay customs are habitual is not essential to the use of those customs as a source of legal conventions. The mercantile customs adopted by courts often reflect the best practice more than the habitual practice. And conventions of international conduct are sometimes enforced as law even when they are not habitually practiced and receive only lip service from many states. In this context, what matters is the conventional, not the habitual dimension of lay custom. Similarly, when all law is said to rest upon the customs of lawyers, the focus is on the habitual dimension of lawyerly custom. Lawyers cannot interpret, reconcile, or apply law without deep reservoirs of tacit know-how. True, the conventional dimension of the custom of lawyers is a major source of procedural law, but the habitual dimension of lawyers' customs underpins all kinds of law.

Similarly, it is often asserted that the growth of law means the decline of custom. But this could refer to two distinct processes: one whereby what is tacit and habitual

---

1. See, for example, James C. Carter, *Law: Its Origin, Growth, and Function* (New York: De Capo Press, 1974) 173.

becomes explicit and stipulated, another whereby informal conventions give way to legally imposed agreements. What we know about human cognition, however, shows that cognitive complexity requires ever greater capacities for habitual routines in information processing and skillful performance: the growing complexity of the interpretation and application of law means a greater role for customary habits in the lives of lawyers.

As for conventions, by focusing merely on their sources, we might well conclude that custom and law are mutually exclusive sources of our conventions, since no convention begins both as informal practice and as stipulated law. On this view, the growth of legal conventions inevitably shrinks the field of customary conventions. But custom is not best thought of merely as a source of law: custom is just as often a consequence of law. Customary conventions do not cease being customs when they become enforced by law. Robert Ellickson shows that the growth of law often stimulates the growth of customary conventions as alternatives to increasingly burdensome legal procedures.[2] Rather, law in many jurisdictions ceases to be law when it loses the support of custom and falls into desuetude. In short, because legal conventions survive only by becoming customary, the growth of law means the growth of custom. Some contemporary scholars of international law argue that there are several ways in which the growth of deliberately stipulated law of treaties and conventions has fostered the profusion of new customary international law. For example, Theodor Meron argues when a large number of states convene to promulgate new rules protecting human rights, a custom of human rights norms emerges which binds even the states not party to the original conventions.[3] In his much controverted view, treaties and conventions can give rise to parallel norms of customary international law, with a wider range of jurisdiction. Indeed, H.W.A. Thirlway argues that custom operates not only in support of written law, but also to supplement written law and even to alter or abolish it.[4] "We have endeavored to show that so far from supplanting customary law, and reducing its field of operation to a minimum, the codifying of great tracts of international law will, on account of the practical and political difficulties of amending multilateral treaties, whether codifying or otherwise, give over the development of international law almost entirely into the hands of custom, operating upon and beyond the codifying treaties."[5] According to these scholars, at least, the growth of law in no way competes with the growth of customary habits or customary conventions.

Those who want to stress the continuity between custom and law will say that both are systems of conventions, that is, agreements to coordinate expectations and conduct. Lon Fuller, for example, argues that customary law does not arise merely from repeated or uniform habits, but from the need for social coordination: "Customary law arises,

---

2. Ellickson, *Order without Law* (Cambridge: Harvard University Press, 1991) Chaps. 3–6.

3. "In the highly codified humanitarian law context, the primary and most obvious significance of a norm's customary character is that the norm binds states that are not parties to the instrument in which that norm is restated. It is, of course, not the treaty norm, but the customary norm with identical content, that binds such states." Theodor Meron, *Human Rights and Humanitarian Norms as Customary Law* (Oxford: Clarendon Press, 1989) 3.

4. Thirlway compares custom to equity, whose relation to written law has been categorized as "equity *secundum legem*, equity *praeter legem*, and equity *contra legem*"; in the same way, he says, custom operates by virtue of the law itself, custom supplements the deficiencies of law, and custom alters or abolishes law. *International Customary Law and Codification* (Leiden: A.W. Sijthoff, 1972) 95.

5. Thirlway, *International Customary Law and Codification* 146.

then, out of situations of human interaction where each participant guides himself by an anticipation of what the other will do and will expect him to do." Customary law, he says, is like contract law: "its underlying principle is a reciprocity of expectations."[6] They argue that law is best understood, not as a command from sovereign to citizen, but as a framework of rules coordinating the legitimate expectations among citizens. On this view, legal conventions do not arise *ex nihilo*, but reinforce, supplement, or abrogate existing customary conventions. The rules of law rarely create new forms of human activity; instead, they tend to regulate and modify ongoing customary human enterprises. The rules of law, then, are more like the rules of etiquette or grammar than like the rules of games or sports.

Those who emphasize continuity will also insist that custom and law regulate conduct most effectively when they rest upon habits. Indeed, Aristotle says that "nomos has no power to command obedience except that of ethos, which can only be given by time, so that readiness to change from old law to new weakens the power of law" (*Pol.* 1269a 20). Aristotle overstates his case here because both custom and law have other ways of encouraging conformity besides the force of habit, namely, social ostracism and legal sanction. Too much change in either custom or law weakens their effectiveness as conventions because it unsettles the expectations upon which we rely in coordinating our plans.

Any particular act of interpretation or application of law must rest largely on tacit customary habits. The cognitive habits by which we interpret and apply law cannot themselves all be reflectively stipulated because they are the means by which we interpret and stipulate. You cannot drive nails if you are focused on how to hold the hammer, and you cannot interpret laws unless you can rely upon a habitual grasp of the meaning of virtually all the terms. For example, it is often asserted that many provisions of business contracts can only be interpreted in relation to the habitual expectations of that business. Lon Fuller famously offered as an example an ordinance prohibiting "vehicles in the park" where parks will be interpreted one way as places of repose and in another way as places of merriment.[7] Apart from the shared customary understandings of human institutions, like parks, interpretation of law would always be indeterminate or arbitrary.

Much of this shared understanding must remain tacit: at any particular occasion, we can bring a part of our tacit understanding to explicit critical reflection, but not all of it at once. Like Neurath's ship at sea, we can focus on this or that problem and make selective repairs, but only by relying implicitly on the soundness of the rest. Or, as Wittgenstein argued, the application of rules to cases cannot be wholly determined by rules without generating an infinite regress. In this view, habitual modes of legal reasoning are as much a part of our law as are the explicit decisions of courts: *cursus curiae est lex curiae*.

Those who emphasize the contrast between custom and law will also develop two independent lines of argument. First, they will draw attention to the difference between legal conventions as positive law—in the sense of deliberately laid down by the sovereign legislator—and customary conventions arising informally from human social practices. But it turns out to be quite difficult to distinguish sharply formal legal conventions from informal customary ones. Voluntarist positivists, like Hobbes and Austin, argued that, since law is a command of the sovereign will, the only organ for directly articulating that will is legislation; the decisions of courts and the customs of merchants could be interpreted as the indirect will of the sovereign with the fiction that "whatever the sovereign

---

6. Fuller, *Anatomy of the Law* (New York: Mentor, 1969) 116.
7. Fuller, *Anatomy of the Law* 93.

permits, he commands." H.L.A. Hart effectively demolished the voluntarist theory of law by showing that laws need not be commands and that persons in authority have reasons for permitting customs even when they disapprove them. Hart famously attempted to distinguish legal from other kinds of conventions on the basis that law involves a union of primary and secondary rules, where the secondary rules are rules about the primary rules, namely, how to identify, apply, and change them.[8]

Whether this adequately distinguishes legal from other conventions is disputed on the basis that the conventions governing private associations, such as sporting clubs, are also unions of primary and secondary rules. For this reason, Joseph Raz distinguishes legal systems from other systems of conventions, not on the basis of differences between types of conventions, but on the basis of the authority claimed by various systems of conventions. What makes legal systems unique, he says, are the claims to be comprehensive, supreme, and open to absorbing other systems of norms.[9]

Some argue that customary conventions arise spontaneously while legal conventions are deliberately made. John Finnis says that customs, unlike laws, are not "made" because "no one sets himself (themselves) to make a custom."[10] But powerful states often precisely set themselves to make customary international law, as the United States did successfully in the Truman Proclamation and as the United States hopes to do by its recent invasions of Afghanistan and Iraq.[11] Now it could be said that even the United States cannot make customary international law unilaterally, unless its conduct is in some sense accepted or taken up by other nations. The invasion of Iraq might well not create a new customary law of preventive war; it might instead provoke clear rejection of the whole doctrine. Precedents similarly do not make new law unless they are taken up in practice; even statutes, in some jurisdictions, can fail through desuetude. So neither custom nor law is made wholly unilaterally: they both require some degree of social uptake.

The effort to distinguish legal from other kinds of conventions has been especially difficult in the case of the common law. Every legal theorist who makes a strong distinction between custom and law must decide whether common law is custom or law. When Thomas Hobbes thinks of common law as custom, he denies it is law: "Custom of itself maketh no law. . . if custom were sufficient to introduce a law, then it would be in the power of every one that is deputed to hear a cause, to make his errors law." Yet Hobbes also offers arguments for why common law might be understood as an indirect command of the sovereign, if the judges are ministers of the sovereign: "in *England* it is the King that makes the Laws, whosoever Pens them. . . ."[12] Jeremy Bentham similarly oscillates between arguing that common law is not law and that common law is judge-made law, that is, judicial legislation. Austin thought that common law represented the tacit will of the

8. Hart, *The Concept of Law*, 2nd ed. (Oxford: Clarendon Press, 1994) Chap. 5.

9. Raz, *The Authority of Law* (Oxford: Clarendon Press, 1979) 116–121.

10. Finnis, *Natural Law and Natural Rights* (Oxford: Clarendon Press) 277. Matt Kramer offers this qualification of Finnis from Shakespeare (Henry V): "Nice customs curtsy to great kings. . . We [kings and queens] are the makers of manners."

11. On the Truman Proclamation, see Byers. *Custom, Power, and the Power of Rules* (Cambridge: Cambridge University Press, 1999) 90–92.

12. Hobbes, *Elements of Law*, Ed. Ferdinand Tönnies, 2nd ed. by M. M. Goldsmith (New York: Barnes and Noble, 1969), II, 10.10, 190; and Hobbes, *A Dialogue Between a Philosopher and a Student of the Common Laws of England*, Ed. Joseph Cropsey (Chicago: University of Chicago Press, 1971) 11, 59.

sovereign because whatever the sovereign permits, he commands. "Now when customs are turned into legal rules by decisions of subject judges, the legal rules which emerge from the customs are *tacit* commands of the sovereign legislature."[13] Austin did, however, reject Bentham's expression "judge-made" law, arguing that the law arising from judicial decisions is different in character from the law made by legislators.

Thus, champions of statute make common law into an indirect mode of legislation, while champions of custom make common law into a kind of custom. St. German said that those customs of the realm neither against the law of God nor against the law of reason are properly called the common law.[14] Blackstone also defined common law in relation to the "unwritten law" of custom, saying that common law included general customs, particular customs, and certain particular laws. But Blackstone goes on to say that only general customs are "the common law, properly so called."[15] Similarly, James Carter argues that Austin's definition of law is actually a definition of legislation: "It properly defines *legislation*—that is, law consciously enacted by men. . . .[16] Despite Carter's definition above of legislation as a kind of law, Carter himself usually strongly contrasts law with legislation and asserts that all law is custom. Friedrich Hayek sharply distinguishes the spontaneous order of markets from the deliberately designed order of organizations; he then argues that common law and custom are examples of spontaneous order while legislation is an example of designed order.[17]

We have seen that among jurists there is very little agreement about the relation of custom to law. Some jurists focus on the habitual, tacit, and spontaneous dimension of custom that they contrast with the explicit, stipulated, and deliberate nature of enacted law while other jurists focus on the conventional dimension of custom that they compare to legal conventions. Custom is thus bafflingly like and unlike law.

But how can we clearly distinguish the stipulated order of law from the spontaneous order of custom if some law is customary? Indeed, some law is not made but found already existing in the practices of a people. Nonetheless, even this customary law has a stipulated dimension, in that courts must set forth general criteria defining which customs will likely be enforced by law. No society can undertake to provide legal enforcement of all customs, so every society must decide which customs will be doubly enforced, both by customary sanctions and by legal sanctions. Customary law therefore refers to that subset of customs deliberately chosen for special enforcement. In this sense, customary law reflects not just the habitual and spontaneous order of custom but also the deliberately stipulated order of law. Moreover, although anyone can stipulate the customs of language into a grammar or the customs of courtesy into a code of manners, not anyone can stipulate which kinds of customs shall be enforced by law. Only someone in a position of authority can stipulate what kind of customs will be treated as lawful. But that authority need not be political authority: an eminent legal scholar, whether Gratian or Savigny,

---

13. Austin, *The Province of Jurisprudence Determined*, Ed. H.L.A. Hart (London: Weidenfeld and Nicolson, 1954) 32.

14. St. German, *Doctor and Student*, Ed. T.F.T. Pluncknett and J. L. Barton (London: Selden Society, 1974) Chap. 7.

15. 1 *Blackstone's Commentaries* Intro. Sec. 3.

16. Carter, *Law: Its Origin, Growth, and Function* (New York: G. P. Putnam, 1907) 182.

17. Hayek, *Law, Legislation, and Liberty*. Vol. 1 (Chicago: University of Chicago Press, 1973) 72–94.

may stipulate principles for the enforcement of custom that are widely accepted among judges.

What kinds of customs tend to be enforced by law? The principles governing the enforcement of custom vary widely across societies. Is there any common core of principles? I think there are a few observations about the legal enforcement of custom that hold generally across societies. To begin with, customs are not enforced piecemeal; instead, every society defines broad domains of conduct in which customs will be legally enforced and domains in which customs are largely shielded from law. Some societies enforce customs of religious observance, others exempt religious customs; some societies enforce customs defining marital responsibilities while others largely shield intimate relations from legal processes. What basis is there for this distinction of domains? Probably, customs will be legally enforced in domains of conduct that occasion the most violent social conflict: often, but not always, customs defining property rights, fair exchange, marriage and kinship, personal injury, and homicide. In these domains, common lawyers have developed three basic criteria for evaluating customs by means of the doctrines of expectation, reliance, and harm.[18] These three tests of custom are applied in a serial order of stringency. Virtually all customs, as conventions, create mutual expectations of conduct. Yet we rely on only some of these expectations in making commitments and when those expectations upon which we have relied are frustrated, we may be materially harmed. So even though virtually all customs give rise to expectations about others' conduct, we rely upon only a small subset of those expectations and our reliance leads us to be harmed in still fewer instances.

Each of these doctrines of expectations, reliance, and harm is subject to normative qualifications that they be reasonable, legitimate, and consistent with public policy or with sound morals. All societies refrain from enforcing customs they regard as unreasonable or immoral. We have no legal right to expect that we can turn back the odometer on a car we are selling, even if that is custom; we have no right to rely upon the promises of a minor, an incompetent, or someone known to be dishonest; we cannot claim to be lawfully harmed if we are cheated by a prostitute. But where we can show legitimate expectation, substantial reliance, and material harm in a particular domain of social life, then courts may well enforce customary rules of exchange or other promises. It is not the case, as John Austin argued, that particular customs are not lawful until a court enforces them; rather, a court enforces them because, as a class of customs meeting established legal criteria, they are regarded as already lawful.

Lawyers often regard custom as a mere "source" of law, along with other sources, such as precedent, authoritative doctrines, treaties, and so forth. In this view, customs are the raw material to be processed into constitutions, statutes, and judicial opinions. But in a deeper sense, law should be regarded as a source of customs. After all, what ultimately matters is the quality of our conduct, not the quality of the laws in our books. Law exists for the sake of better conduct; our conduct does not exist for the sake of better laws. True, not all of our conduct is customary, but in a complex world with many competing demands upon our limited capacities for attention, we want as much of our conduct to become "second nature" as possible. If we were to wax Hegelian, we would say that law

---

18. See, for example, James C. Carter's discussion of admiralty law in *Law: Its Origin, Growth, and Function*, 70f and 271ff.

is one way for custom to come to self-understanding and that law is one vehicle by which custom regulates its own evolution. Just as grammarians bring our tacit knowledge of language into explicit focus, so lawyers bring our implicit knowledge of custom into explicit focus. And just as good grammarians strive both to describe and to improve our linguistic customs, so do good lawyers. Many of our customs began as laws and law is most successful when it becomes customary. No doubt many grammarians and lexicographers see customary language as merely a source of formal grammars and dictionaries. But we know that grammars and lexicons should serve living languages, just as law should serve living customs. Just as it is better to speak good English by customary habit, rather than by constant recourse to lexicons, so it is better to conform to good laws by customary habit, than by constant recourse to lawyers. But so long as both laws and grammars aim to improve customary usage, there will always be some gap between the law as written and the conduct regulated.

In the case of desuetude, jurists disagree about whether the customs of the people or of legal officials are decisive. Thomas Aquinas, Francisco Suárez, and Hans Kelsen developed bottom-up theories of desuetude: if the people cease to obey a law, then the law falls into desuetude.[19] But contemporary legal positivists such as Matthew Kramer argue that what is necessary and sufficient for desuetude is that legal officials cease to enforce a law, quite apart from any customs of the people.[20] The customs of the people may be sufficient to cause a law to fall into desuetude, but they are not necessary. I think that Kramer is right that the customs of legal officials are decisive for desuetude, but in practice the reason that legal officials cease to enforce a law is usually because popular custom no longer supports the law. Legal officials, after all, are themselves citizens who are often democratically accountable to their fellow citizens, so we would expect them to be responsive to shifts in popular customs. We are witnessing those shifts today in the enforcement of laws against sodomy, gay marriage, and marijuana: legal officials are ceasing to enforce laws that are rapidly losing support in popular custom. Not all jurisdictions formally recognize desuetude, but all jurisdictions experience the desuetude of law in practice. As Pindar said long ago, custom truly is king.

Many heirs of the Enlightenment today think that law and custom are incompatible, that social progress means the replacement of irrational custom by rational law. In this view, rational reflection in general ought to replace subrational prejudice. But our choice is not between reason and prejudice or between custom and law. Prejudice and custom are psychologically and socially necessary parts of human life: most of our knowledge and skill must remain tacit because of our severe cognitive limitations. Instead of hoping to replace prejudice with reason or custom with law, we should instead attempt to make our prejudices and our customs more decent.

19. "*Desuetudo ist eine gleichsam negative Gewohnheit, deren wesentliche Funktion darin besteht, die Geltung einer bestehende Norm aufzuheben*." Kelsen, *Reine Rechtslehre* (Wien: Franz Deuticke, 1960), 220.

20. Matt Kramer has made this point to me repeatedly in conversation.

INDEX

www.ingramcontent.com/pod-product-compliance
Ingram Content Group UK Ltd.
Pitfield, Milton Keynes, MK11 3LW, UK
UKHW020923170926
475595UK00031B/32

9 780199 370627